# Art is for Children

How parents and teachers can help
develop a child's natural ability in art

## EUGENIA M. OOLE

**AUGSBURG** Publishing House • Minneapolis

ART IS FOR CHILDREN

ART CREDITS

*Front Cover:*
A HAPPY DAY IN SUMMER — tempera
Stephen Schultis
Grade 2
Prairie Village, KS

*Back cover:*
HAPPY BIRTHDAY, DADDY — crayon and marker
Sheila Jane Gohil
Kindergarten
Fulton, MO

UNTITLED COLLAGE
Keith Colston
Grade 3
Inkster, MI

POLICE STATION — felt marker
Nathan Aune
Kindergarten
Northfield, MN

SWEET GIRL — tissue, yarn, paper collage
Sarah Johnson
Grade 3
Dearborn Heights, MI

UNIDENTIFIED FLYING OBJECT
Steve Schudlich
Dearborn, MI

# Contents

# Introduction

HAVE YOU EVER WATCHED a five year old busily painting at an easel? Many years ago I observed an incident I have never forgotten. As the building art teacher, I had gone to the kindergarten to discuss a school project with the teacher and found her talking with a young mother whose son would be entering kindergarten in the fall. As I waited, I noted that the child was painting an entire sheet of 18 by 24 inch paper all blue. He was so engrossed in painting at the easel that he didn't even notice my entering the room.

His mother was obviously impatient as she shifted from one foot to the other, but the teacher knowingly kept her involved in conversation until she observed that the child had finished painting. Only then did she move toward the child and offer to roll the painting carefully as soon as it was dry enough to take home. When he looked up with a big smile and said he didn't want it, his mother grabbed his hand and made a hasty departure.

I could not follow them so can only guess what she might have said to her son. Did she say, "Now why in the world did you have to finish that if you didn't even want it?" or "Why did you waste all that blue paint?" or "Why didn't you paint a *real* picture?" or some equally derogatory question reflecting her irritation with the delay.

What her son really needed to hear was a comment, such as, "How nice of Miss J. to let you paint today," or "Would you like to paint again?" or "I know you will enjoy kindergarten next year," or "That really was fun, wasn't it?"

How many adults recognize that a young child needs to explore and experience art in diverse forms with adult support rather than criticism and ridicule? This child's reaction to his first experience of painting at an easel was a perfectly natural and normal one. He was happily discovering what paint can do on paper, and that *he* could control the brush in covering the page. He felt no concern for making a product, a picture of something, or of pleasing anyone but himself. And once having accomplished that to his own satisfaction, he had no further interest in the painting.

During my lifetime career in art education, I have learned much from children that I am eager to share with all adults— parents, grandparents, aunts, uncles, teachers, group leaders— everyone whose lives are intimately connected with children. It has been observed repeatedly that much of what children experience in their preschool and early school years lays the foundation for their entire lives. We cannot afford to neglect any aspect of growth during these formative years and art experiences are vital to the total development of every individual.

In the pages that follow, I shall endeavor to provide a greater understanding of the importance of visual expression to children's total growth, the range of experiences as seen through the eyes of children that provide ideas for them to express, the materials appropriate for their art, and the basic art elements and principles that guide all art, as children put it all together in *their own* way. Adults will be given helpful suggestions on how to talk with children, how to stimulate them without over-directing them, how to relate to the world of art, and how to share the resulting creative experiences enjoyably and profitably.

A final section will provide ready references to materials and processes, not necessarily costly ones, which may be most effectively used. However, the reader is urged to use this information only in the context of the preceding chapters, not by itself alone.

Art *is* for children in every sense of the word for it is a vital key to their complete development.

# 1

# The Role of Art in Children's Total Growth

HAVE YOU EVER TRIED TO PREDICT THE FUTURE? Can you even guess what the world will be like fifteen or twenty years hence when the youngsters of today are ready to take their places as functioning members of their society? When we recall the rapid developments we have seen in our own lifetime, we can be certain that vast changes will continue to occur in coming decades. We cannot possibly conceive of every situation children will face during their lifetime, but as responsible adults we recognize our obligation for preparing them, to the best of our ability, to face *their* world as effectively as possible.

Because the education of children begins in infancy, it must be started long before they enter schools, should continue parallel to school experiences, and extend throughout their lifetime. Parents and all adults who contact children in their formative years have important roles in providing for their continuous total development.

Most parents show great excitement over children's first words and first steps. But how do they react to children's first scribbles on a piece of paper? Many shrug it off with a mental note, "My child isn't an artist any more than I am." If you have

ever reacted this way, you are probably unaware that a child's first scribble is just as important as that first word or step. Each aspect of development goes through progressive stages. A word becomes a phrase, a sentence, then a paragraph as reading, writing and language skills progress. That first step moves through walking, running, skipping and similar motor skills toward control of one's body. The scribble moves systematically through stages of artistic growth equally important to total development as we shall examine later in greater detail.

One of the chief reasons why adults feel insecure about understanding children's artistic expression is because art has no "right" or "wrong" form. Adults recognize the specific symbols used in alphabet and number systems. They know there are correct ways to spell words, construct sentences, and develop paragraphs. Even the letter forms used in printing and writing have acceptable standard forms. Arithmetic problems may be quickly checked for correctness. But how can we understand and interpret the symbols children use in developing their own visual symbolism? And why is this so important to all children's total development?

In order to understand these and related questions, we need first to look briefly at background information that can help to clarify and guide adults in recognizing the importance of art in the lives of *all* persons. History records examples of artistic expression, such as drawings by

prehistoric people on the walls of caves, long before noting any evidence of written or spoken language. Artifacts found at ancient sites reveal objects of human ornamentation such as brooches and necklaces, expertly made pottery and tools, and small sculptured forms. People who lived many centuries ago showed consummate skill and artistry in constructing both utilitarian and decorative objects. And much of our knowledge about these early civilizations — Ancient Egypt, Mesopotamia, Crete, India, China, others — has been learned from their art. If art has played such a vital role for centuries, its importance certainly cannot be denied today.

Looking back to the early centuries of the Christian era, we find that the art and architecture of the church played a significant role in teaching people about the Bible and the Christian faith. For example, the symbol for the fish identified believers covertly when public admission of the faith would have meant certain persecution. Many of the symbols devised to insure secrecy have come down through the ages with countless others added in succeeding centuries to serve in educating people in the faith. Throughout Europe in the Middle Ages and during the Renaissance, people learned the teachings of the Bible by seeing great art repeatedly in frescoes, mosaics, reliefs, sculptures, stained glass windows, plus

numerous other objects long before books were printed or they were able to read. If one studies other religions, such as Buddhism or Mohammedanism, one finds similar use of symbolism to promote the faith, but each distinctly related to its own philosophy and beliefs. Primitive civilizations have used unique art forms as adjuncts of their religious ceremonies also. Symbolism, as a pervasive quality of art, is likewise significant to our understanding of children's art.

The importance of art as communication has already been alluded to in noting our knowledge of history and the use of symbolism in teaching religious beliefs to people unable to read and write. But the communication value of art goes beyond such measures. Today we live in a *visual* world. Most children today do not know a world without television. Advanced technology makes it an everyday experience to witness world events as they occur—man walking on the moon, the assassination of a president, the funeral of a world leader, as well as both natural and man-made catastrophes. In an age of instant photography when what one sees can be recorded and transmitted immediately, the expression of deep personal feelings through art assumes even greater importance. Both the mature artist and the young child use symbols in personal and significant ways to communicate sensitive inner feelings. It is interesting to note that the artists of communist countries are forced by their governments to be highly realistic and essentially photographic in their art because of the fear their leaders have that abstract symbolism may contain hidden meanings. Children often develop their own visual symbols to a complex level in interpreting and reacting to experiences, events, and feelings of today's visual world.

As we look at the increasing complexity of our technological society, we cannot begin to anticipate the nature of the work or the kinds of jobs today's children will ultimately hold. Much is heard about the importance of basic skills which are usually interpreted as including reading, writing, and arithmetic, or in common parlance, the three R's. In these terms, art could well be called the fourth R for visual learning cannot be overlooked. Could space scientists develop a space capsule capable of taking people to the moon and back with only verbal skills? Many famous scientists credit their creative thinking capacity to a combination of visual and verbal skills. We cannot predict accurately what directions our children will go in realizing their life goals, but we can prepare them more effectively if we provide ample development of visual as well as verbal skills. Every thinking adult today wants the next generation capable of thinking creatively and acting responsibly.

In recent years psychologists and educators have been concerned about studying aspects of creativity as found not only in those engaged in the various arts but also as revealed by scientists, engineers, mathematicians and people in other fields. Likewise recent interest has been shown in the way differentiation of the brain into left and right hemispheres plays a role in learning. It is generally concluded that the left hemisphere controls those skills associated with verbal and mathematical aspects while the right hemisphere governs visual-spatial abilities. Studies are far from conclusive but there is strong belief that the arts have far-reaching effects on both physical and intellectual development, the neglect of which would seriously impair the ability of human beings to perceive their world completely.

Certainly not the least of our concerns should be in the improvement of a child's self-image. One does not need to search far to find reports of children who gained confidence through the arts. Children with reading problems have been observed repeatedly to master reading skills because of interest in some aspect of art. Many young children, if encouraged, will illustrate their ideas long before they are able to write about them. Some educators are finding great success through an arts-centered curriculum in which all other subjects are learned through the arts.

Our purpose here is not to review comprehensively the extensive literature in the field. For those who wish to delve more deeply into various aspects, there are plenty of sources available. It is our intent at this point simply to verify the fact that art is indeed *basic* in the education of all persons. We shall now turn our attention to ways that adults can encourage art expression in children during both preschool years and the early grades in school.

Those who have studied the way children all over the world respond to art experiences have identified certain clearly recognizable stages of development. Although the terms used to identify each may vary and the average time span for each may differ according to a child's experience, the overriding similarities are evident. In order to help adults recognize these pervasive stages, we shall identify each and describe it briefly. Educators believe that every person, regardless of age, will experience essentially the same developmental process, however brief, when encountering an art experience for the first time.

When children are first given simple materials—paper, crayons, clay and the like—they *manipulate* them or *scribble* with them. If adults were handed a ball of moist clay for the first time, what would each do with it? Will they just look at it? Probably each will squeeze it, poke it, push holes in it. This is manipulation, though it may be very brief, before that person starts forming or shaping it in some fashion. Very young children will grasp crayons in their fists and scribble back and forth or in circular fashion. Gradually, as they gain control, their scribbles or balls of clay take on crude shapes. This is a perfectly normal reaction which should not be hampered by adults. It is important to note that if ample paper and working space are not provided, the child may naively choose the wall for his scribbles.

A significant step can be noted when the child names the scribble. Adult acceptance is crucial. No matter how crude the form appears to the adult, it must be recognized as a vital step in the developmental process. Generally, children will begin to develop their own crude symbols for those objects, persons, feelings which are important to them. At no point should any adult attempt to correct such a symbol or show the child how to draw something. The role of the adult must be only that of encouragement, of acceptance, and of stimulating the experiences and ideas behind the drawing or other art form. It is the child's development that is important, not the product.

When children are encouraged to develop their own symbols, they will often evolve amazingly complex interpretations of their own personal experiences. As adults we must accept the fact that the *symbolic stage* represents the world through a child's not an adult's eyes. As we learn to appreciate each child's very personal reactions, we will experience the charm and the unique qualities so characteristic of genuine child art which no adult can match or even imitate successfully.

During the symbolic stage, color is often highly emotional rather than real, size of objects portrayed will relate to their importance rather than to actuality, perspective in the adult sense will be absent, and more than one event may be shown simultaneously. As children's personal experiences become richer and more meaningful, they will evolve increasingly more effective ways of portraying them. Gradually their expression *may* become more real in appearance, but realism, as such, should not be considered the "best" or "only" significant goal. We can observe some children who develop a sense of minute detail as they pursue a special interest. I have known children who love to draw elaborate boats, airplanes, and other vehicles in accurate detail. A third grader in one of my classes once drew an instrument panel of an airplane from memory and explained all the dials to me. He was an avid reader of *Popular Mechanics*. Other children draw imaginary space ships, other planets, and fantasy ideas with similar detail. On the other hand, many children will continue to maintain a naive, child-like approach but will show more intricately conceived ideas in response to richer experiences.

A word should be said about age patterns in relation to these stages of artistic development. However, in every case one must take into account the child's previous experience rather than observing age levels as rigidly specific. Generally, the scribbling stage will range from two to four years of age. If children have frequent experiences with art materials, they may begin to name their scribbles very soon. Others who have no previous experiences may be scribbling at age five, even after entering kindergarten, but will usually move through the naming of scribbling very quickly and begin developing crude personal symbols. If adult approaches are not forced, children will continue to evolve increasingly more elaborate symbols until ages seven or eight, or even longer. As will be pointed out later, it is important to increase the experience level of children allowing them to develop their expression freely. Greater feeling toward reality has no fixed point and should not be expected to develop automatically in all children. The line between symbolism and reality may be difficult to make and is less important in the long run than the personal quality of the expression. Each child should be respected for uniqueness rather than for uniformity of expression.

Parents often raise the question, "How can we tell if our child is gifted in art?" In very young children it is very difficult to determine. The child who appears to be unusually capable in art may not maintain such apparent ability whereas some who show less potential at a very young age blossom more fully later. Parents should be alert to providing all possible avenues for creative expression, giving encouragement, and sharing experiences with *all* children so that the fullest benefits possible may occur. By providing an accepting climate, each child will have freedom to develop.

Likewise, it is important to recognize the needs of handicapped children for art expression. Regardless of the precise nature of the handicaps present in children, it is essential to permit the fullest creative development in every child. Often art experiences can provide the element of success so vital to the self-image of a handicapped child. The utmost of patience is necessary, for it may take a handicapped child considerably longer to accomplish any task. I recall a very active group of first graders who developed their own circus. At their insistence, I helped them make a big clown, a little clown, and a giraffe they could sit on—all from papier mâché. In addition, they put on their own circus acts. Patty suffered from convulsions but was an eager member of the circus troop. Because of her inability to control her movements readily, she chose to be a clown and carried out her role eagerly. Later, when the children drew and painted pictures of their circus, Patty made herself as a clown. To the general viewer, her drawing appeared crude, but I knew that it represented supreme effort, for it was the first time she had really tried to make anything specific in a drawing. Patty desperately needed to do this for herself, to sense that she could do it. The other children sensed this intuitively and commented, "Isn't Patty's picture nice," and "I like Patty's clown." All of this benefit would have been lost if an unthinking adult had decided, "Patty is handicapped, so she cannot participate." Determination is a thing many handicapped people possess and we must never break that tremendous will to accomplishment. Our assistance to *their* efforts must be given only when requested by the child, never because we could do it quicker, easier, or with better "results."

During my early teaching years, I learned an important lesson from a first grade child born with only short stubs of arms and no hands. Again and again I watched him dump his crayons on the table, then, gripping a color between his two stubs, stand up and draw vigorously. I saw him cut with scissors, though crudely, if I held the paper when he requested it. And the most amazing thing was to see him model a small bowl in clay quicker than his classmates. One of the other children suddenly blurted out, though she hadn't even touched her ball of clay, "How can Bobby make a bowl when he has no hands?" Then seeing how vigorously he was working, she quickly added, "I guess I'd better get started!" After seeing Bobby's determination and pride in his accomplishment, for he loved art, I knew I would forever devote my energies to helping others recognize the importance of art for handicapped individuals. No matter how long it takes or how crude the result, we must help handicapped children gain independence and never succumb to doing it for them.

Children of different ages within a family or neighborhood can create difficulties unless one is alert. Young children should be encouraged at all times to work in their own way, imitating neither older siblings nor adults. Parents have an important role in helping the older brother or sister appreciate the younger child. By demonstrating clearly their acceptance of *each* child's unique efforts, parents can avoid feelings of inadequacy or superiority as the case may be. Parents pave the way by insisting that older children are not to do the work for the younger ones. If necessary, parents may need to confide in the older ones and if available, they may bring out work done earlier by the older children when they were younger to heighten their appreciation of a younger sibling's efforts. Another way to avoid unfortunate comparisons is to generate different forms of art expression for diverse age levels. A fairly safe rule to follow is that if we, as adults, must do the work for a child, then it is beyond that child's present scope.

The stage has now been set for encouraging children's visual skills to develop. Helping children experience new things as they react excitedly to the world around them can be very satisfying to adults as well. We have already noted that parents should not show children *how* to express themselves visually but have identified a very significant role for them to perform. From the earliest years forward, children need to be guided in a vast array of personal experiences ranging from simple, everyday events to more elaborate ones. Sensitive adult-child sharing is the key leading to significant learning. Give children exciting things to say and they will find ways to express them.

# 2

# Seeing the World
# Through Children's Eyes

CHILDREN ARE NATURALLY CURIOUS. When left to their own devices, young children's curiosity may lead them into situations that are potentially dangerous. All too often we hear of children having accidents or of becoming lost after straying too far from familiar areas. Unfortunately, not all such adventures have a happy ending. Yet, the inquisitiveness of children needs to be cultivated in order to build their sensitivity to the world around them. Obviously, adults cannot be with children every moment but there are many ways in which they can guide children in the kinds of experiences that will build a foundation for future learning and growth.

A few years ago I went to visit a friend in a neighboring town. When I arrived in late morning, I found her busily preparing lunch and her four-year-old son was setting the table. It was fascinating to watch him climb on a step stool to remove dishes and silver from the cupboard, then carefully take them piece-by-piece to the dining room table. After he appeared to have finished his job, his mother came to help him check. Then I heard him say, "Will the lady drink coffee?" With her answer, he returned to the kitchen to get another cup and saucer. Apparently satisfied, he went outside to play until lunch time.

His mother, an experienced teacher, confided in me that she could do the job more easily and more quickly herself, but she felt the importance of helping her son learn how to accept responsibility for simple family chores. His obvious pride in the recognition adults made of his contribution proved her purpose readily. But how many times do parents overlook such simple experiences in the lives of their children?

Even very young children need to become conscious of their importance as family members. Sharing simple tasks can be a very significant means of building each child's self-image. Putting away toys, hanging up clothes, running simple errands can be quickly accomplished by young children as they build basic habits. As these children grow older, particularly if there are younger children in the family, they can assume greater responsibilities. If purposeful activity is encouraged at home, it can be continued readily at school with increased complexity. Establishing a time for work and a time for play can help children grow to appreciate lifetime responsibilities. What is more, these experiences will become the themes for all forms of creative expression engaged in by children. The child who responds eagerly to family experiences will never lack ideas for drawings, paintings or other forms of artistic expression.

As soon as children begin to name their scribbles, it becomes apparent that their personal experiences are important to them. When adults show eagerness to share the child's art expression, they will hear responses typified by the following samples:

> "This is me helping Daddy rake the yard"
> "I went to the grocery store with Mommy"
> "I like to play with my dog, Spot"
> "This is me eating my breakfast"
> "I am putting my doll to bed"

Parents who wish to establish healthful and constructive habits in their children can often capitalize on children's enthusiasm for artistic expression. By exhibiting interest and praising a child's painting or drawing, parents can establish their children's habits more vividly than by merely discussing them verbally. It is essential to encourage children's visual and verbal expression by taking time to listen to what they wish to tell you and by sharing their enthusiasm wholeheartedly.

During the early years, the child is the center of all activity. Any verbal description is apt to start with *me* and extends to *me* and *my* in relation to all events. As a child grows older, the enthusiastic but ungrammatical "Me and My . . . " will give way to the more acceptable, "My . . . and I. . . . " One should not be critical of the language, but accept the obvious meaning, for correcting the young child's language at this stage may only cause frustration. As family experiences extend beyond the home, children who have gained self-confidence can accept their roles in group situations more readily.

For many children, the earliest experiences outside the home will be related to religious activities. Before children attend school or learn to read, they may participate in group activities in a church or synagogue environment. The love of God will be exemplified to them in many ways before the significance of scriptural knowledge can be grasped. Through simple stories, music, dramatic play, they may encounter children of diverse backgrounds for the first time. Learning to become sensitive to people outside their own families may be a vital aspect of this experience for children. Helping children express visually as well as verbally those things for which they are thankful and which show God's love can be a very important aspect of their earliest spiritual life. Such expressions must be created in their own personal way, never prescribed by adults.

We cannot emphasize enough the importance of family participation in experiences involving young children. Through togetherness, children learn basic values which will be important guides to future living. Through their very personal expression, however crude in appearance, children exercise their abilities to make choices, to distinguish right from wrong, and

to express deep inner feelings which might not be possible verbally with their limited vocabularies. Unqualified acceptance of the child's own personal expression is crucial. We must never tell a child what to express visually or how to express it. We must stand ready to understand children as we interpret their expression and give constant encouragement to them to continue.

For some children, nursery school will precede formal school experience. Parents need to be aware constantly of the nature of children's school activities in order to expand family experiences in complementary fashion. No school can do everything and the diversity of interests among children makes it impossible to meet the individual needs of each child completely. Early school experiences in art should permit the child complete freedom of personal expression. Formalized or dictated lessons have no place. The child who has a wealth of personal experiences to draw from will never be at loss to decide what to express. When children enter kindergarten or first grade, as the case may be, amplification and deepening of experiences will add stimulation to creative expression. But again, no school, no teacher can provide all. Family and related institutions continue to play an important role in formulating children's background experiences enabling them to take full advantage of their total education both in and out of school.

Nature provides some of the most valuable resources for learning for every human being. Although children learn many facts about the wonders of nature in school, they cannot gain full understanding inside a classroom. One must experience nature directly to appreciate it completely. The possibilities for family enjoyment are endless, but we can suggest a few examples as guides. For those who live in climates with changing seasons, life is governed by the progression from winter to spring, to summer, to fall, and back again to winter. The effect of the seasons upon growth cycles of plants, trees, food crops, insects, birds, animals becomes a wonderful revelation to children.

There is endless fascination in watching seeds germinate and push thin shoots up through the soil, of watching trees bud, blossom, leaf out and bear fruit, of seeing a butterfly emerge from a cocoon, of observing the returning flights of birds, the hatching of young birds or chickens from eggs, and following the birth and development of baby animals. Tropical climates produce growth patterns that are equally exciting to observe. Deserts, mountains, forests, farm lands, all parts of the world offer unique opportunities both to observe growth and to respect life itself. When adults take time to help children discover these phenomena, both the children and the adults reap benefits.

Another aspect of nature which can stimulate both adults and children relates to the distinctly visual qualities present. We can all thrill to a glorious sunrise or flaming

sunset. We can marvel at the grandeur of rugged mountains, a plunging waterfall, the arching of a brilliant rainbow, a river rushing over rocks or gliding placidly through fields, the sweep of winds through trees, waves beating upon the shore, the fury of a thunderstorm, or the calm beauty of reflections on a lake. Do you recall your own fascination in watching clouds? Everyone can be quickly stirred by finding forms in the clouds—a dragon, a castle, a cowboy on a horse, someone dancing, a huge face, or the figment of one's wildest imagination. We can view a vast panorama or we can glimpse intimate bits of nature with full awareness that, in the words of the Psalmist, "The earth is the Lord's, and the fulness thereof;" and that we can share it together.

Sometimes the grandeurs of nature can be frightening to younger children unless adults help them to develop a fuller understanding. I recall that a mother whose daughter was afraid of thunder and lightning storms helped her overcome her fear in a simple way. She encouraged her daughter to observe a bird's nest in a nearby tree and recognize that God was looking after each little baby bird in the nest. Because she capitalized on her daughter's love for birds and animals, she got her to look out the window to observe the nest instead of hiding during a storm. From then on, she forgot her fear of storms.

Much can be learned by observing the minutiae as well as the great spectacles of nature. Adults can help children to observe minute aspects of nature that are easily overlooked. Children can be guided in their identification of differences among the shapes of common leaves, of the textures of tree bark, of the characteristic form of familiar trees, and in learning their names. Watching both flowering plants and vegetables as they develop from tiny shoots to maturity can be exciting. Keeping track as birds build their nests, hatch the eggs, pull up worms to feed the baby birds, then seeing the baby birds learn to fly can be exciting to share. Observation of water in every form—in a puddle or vast lake, in a rushing stream or turbulent waterfall, frozen in an icicle or on a skating rink, calm as glass or rolling in huge waves—offers constant variety. Children are fascinated by woolly caterpillars inching along a twig, a tiny ladybug, a filmy dragonfly, a fluttering butterfly, or other insect. Not to be overlooked are the qualities both visual and tactile in a stone washed smooth by water, the wood grain of an old weathered plank, cracks in old pavement, grass bent in the wind, sand pushed by waves along a beach. Helping children learn to enjoy these aspects visually without harming or disturbing them is a step toward full recognition of our reliance upon nature and dependence upon God for our well-being.

Part of the pattern of family life is the observance of holidays and significant days. Unfortunately, the commercialization of major holidays has brought an abundance of stereotyped objects and symbols which tend to overpower the more delightfully significant expressions of children. For many children, the true meaning of Christmas is stifled by Santa Clauses on every corner and in every department store. When parents take the time to share with children the Bible stories related to the birth of Christ, they will be rewarded by uniquely personal drawings, paintings and other expressions as only children can produce them. The feeling precedes the expression and that cannot be created artificially. The same can be said about tree and home decorations. Children need encouragement to develop unique ideas commensurate with their own level of development instead of being forced to imitate adult level forms. Genuine child art has no match; naive simplicity of child expression can be far more meaningful than the most sophisticated approach which is copied.

Adults need to avoid undue attention to such commercially dominated holidays as Valentine's Day, St. Patrick's Day, Mother's Day, Father's Day, and Halloween. Only when children are mature enough to develop their own conception of such special days should they be encouraged to produce greeting cards or decorations. The use of patterns causes more harm than good. If children understand the significance of these holidays, then they can be provided with materials and encouraged to create their *own* original forms of expression. The simplest original Valentine or Mother's Day card a young child produces not only benefits that child's development, but also offers adults a truer insight into the child's personal feelings. No commercial card can match genuine personal expression.

A special caution should be raised in relation to days of distinctly historical significance. If all we can transmit to a child about George Washington is that he cut down a cherry tree, we are only perpetuating a dubious myth. It is far better to wait until children understand enough about heroes to be able to choose for themselves what to express and how to express it, than to force trite replicas. Thanksgiving is a deeply significant day to all Americans but it has been greatly abused. Instead of overpopulating the world with paper turkeys, we need to reemphasize consideration for those things for which we give thanks. Ask a child to tell you what he is most thankful for and you may be pleasantly surprised by the maturity of the reply.

Shortly after the close of World War II, I discussed with a first grade class things for which we were most thankful prior to their drawing pictures of these things. When we looked at and discussed their pictures, we learned such preferences as:

"I'm glad I have a good school and nice teachers"
"I'm thankful for a warm house and good parents"
"I'm so glad I have a new baby brother"
"I'm happy for my very own puppy"

But the most revealing answer came from a little girl who had just entered our school the week before. Her reply was, "I'm thankful for enough food to eat. You know many little boys and girls in the world go to bed hungry." The full significance of her expression came when I learned later that the family had been in government service abroad and had only recently succeeded with great difficulty in getting out of an Iron Curtain country via Vienna. They had experienced hunger firsthand.

Such personal expressions reveal thinking on the part of individual children rather than adherence to trite and overworked themes. For too long we have emphasized the Pilgrim and Indian theme even though little children can scarcely understand the true significance, and historical research is casting doubt upon the authenticity of many aspects of the oft-repeated tales. Even the dress generally depicted for both Pilgrims and Indians scarcely fits the November climate of New England. If we believe it is important to give thanks to God annually for our blessings, then we should emphasize personal significance in the present rather than replicating the past.

Easter, one of the most important days in the Christian calendar, is generally more difficult for young children to understand fully. In the case of very young children especially, parents should probably stress most the aspect of new life which is consistent with the season. Although the egg symbol has deep significance, it has been given emphasis along with the Easter bunny that is difficult to overcome. Perhaps the best suggestion to adults is to let a child's expression take its own course, watching for evidence of deeper understanding before attempting to stimulate new ideas.

When we observe carefully how individual children react to their situations, we can learn a great deal. Some children have such strong personal interests that they refuse to be sidetracked. I recall a particular first grader who fits this concept precisely. John lived along the main street of a community through which a great deal of heavy truck traffic passed en route to Chicago. This was before the era of the fully developed interstate highway system. John was fascinated by the huge semi trucks he saw daily and drew them constantly with amazing detail. When the other children were expressing things about which they were thankful, John drew his usual semi. When finished, he brought it to me with the question, "Do you know what is in it?" Before I could even venture an answer, he announced, "Turkeys." The pattern was repeated in December when he informed me that his semi was loaded with Christmas trees. As the Easter season approached, he handed me his picture one day with a smile but not a word. You've guessed it! This time his semi had in huge letters across the side, "EGGS." I have always felt that John acted very deliberately and had learned exactly how to get around adults who did not appreciate his interest. Because I showed my respect for his efforts, he always showed me his pictures willingly. We should add that in due time, John shifted his attention to many other interests.

Most communities have their own particular places of interest to which parents can take their children. Family outings to parks, playgrounds, ball games, parades, carnivals, festivals, fairs, woods, swimming beaches, zoos, museums, band concerts, and many others create memorable experiences for children. When people are asked to recall special events from their childhood, many will quickly name the experiences related to family outings. The number of times that children draw pictures about such excursions substantiates the great significance of these experiences in their early lives. Visits to grandparents or other relatives are frequently remembered vividly. The variety of things children recall from such trips, whether taken with their families or with school groups, will be revealed again and again in subsequent art expression. The child who has visited a zoo will be much more willing not only to draw pictures of the zoo itself, but will also extend the experience into paintings depicting a jungle, Noah's Ark, Daniel in the Lions' Den, or other equally relevant themes.

Firsthand experience is vital to children's art expression. Several years ago, I accompanied a group of urban first graders on their first visit to a dairy farm. Their excitement was so great that most of them were reluctant to leave. They were allowed to pet the calves, watched cows being milked by hand and with milking machines, saw the huge barns and pasture areas. And of course, they loved milk and cookies provided by the farmer's wife. When they reached their classroom, their teacher wisely let them choose art materials and go to work immediately. The ensuing work period was as exciting as the resulting drawings, for their enthusiasm was bubbling over. One little boy insisted on a large piece of wrapping paper on which he drew a cow larger than himself. Others drew cows being milked, cows coming in from the pasture, and innumerable other aspects of their exciting day in the country. But the prize interpretation was a huge cow with a milk bag at both ends! On similar occasions I have observed children so engrossed in painting or drawing a vivid experience that they have employed full sound effects in the process.

Trips to museums and art galleries are important in the lives of children. Just as adults become weary when trying to view too much in a single visit, so children are apt to tire quickly. Short trips to see only limited examples of art, artifacts, other objects will yield the most productive results. I remember an adult, when discussing whether it is better for children to grow up in a city, small town, or rural area, stated emphatically her preference for growing up in New York City. Her chief reason was her regular visits to the Metropolitan Museum of Art. Her professional career was in the field of biology but she valued highly her extensive childhood experience with art. More suggestions will be given in a later chapter about the most effective use of museum visits for children.

Parents who analyze their own particular life-style will be able to add innumerable other ways they can help their children relate to the world around them. Taking the time to plan for such simple yet vital experiences will yield important results. The crucial point is that parents are helping children learn to see for themselves and, in the process, are building valuable means of establishing their self-confidence. As adults, we can never be sure what will impress children most or what uses children will make of their experiences. But of this we can be certain, that without direct experiences, children have little to express. Discussing and sharing children's reactions to experiences, encouraging expression of their ideas, and accepting wholeheartedly what the child does will pay rich dividends along their developmental paths. In the process, children will begin to become aware of their dependence on others and their need to relate to other human beings throughout their lives. Parents who show respect for and deep enjoyment of their environment provide excellent role models.

One final example demonstrates clearly that adults cannot predict with any certainty what a child will glean from an experience. A second grade class in a rather small town visited the fire station run by the volunteer fire department. I did not accompany them but learned from their classroom teacher that they saw the fire trucks, hoses, living quarters, fire pole and other details. When they came to the art room the next day, I suggested that they might like to show me what they observed on their trip. Contrary to what I thought they might choose to paint, I observed that every last child painted either a raging fire, a fire truck racing to the scene of a fire, or firemen battling a fire. There had been no fire for at least six weeks prior to their trip, but each child was stimulated to produce an action painting triggered by their visit and previous recollections. No child depicted any aspect of the actual visit. As I looked at one little girl's painting of two firemen dressed in heavy coats and fire-hats and holding a large hose between them, she commented very seriously, "That hose gets awfully heavy when it's full of water."

# 3

# Exciting Surprises in Store

HAVE YOU EVER OBSERVED children putting aside expensive toys for seemingly dubious objects of their own contrivance? It is often difficult for adults to understand why children choose a scrubby teddy bear, a battered doll, a rickety wagon in preference to a brand new one. If one observes children at play, one soon discovers how imaginative and ingenious they are in their make-believe world when a piece of crumpled paper is a lion or a person from Mars, a packing box is an airplane or a space ship, and the child is king of all he surveys.

To keep these fertile young minds flexible and to encourage every possible avenue for creativity should be the aim of every adult. There can be no single method, for the very essence of creative thinking requires flexibility of approach, fluency of expression, and above all, individual integrity. These qualities are important to every human being and may be developed through diverse channels. The scientist, the engineer, the mathematician, the business executive, the educator—all need to develop creative thinking capacities just as much as those for whom the need seems more obvious—the artist, the writer, the composer, the playwright, the architect, the choreographer.

We cannot claim that art is the sole means of producing creative thinkers, but art experiences can spark more creatively among young children than many other experiences. For example, one would scarcely place a young child in a scientific laboratory with dangerous chemicals, but one can encourage that same child to experiment with safe art materials to discover the potentials in each. A child can learn to solve basic construction problems with paper, cardboard, wood scraps and other harmless materials long before the tools and materials of the architect or engineer are available or practical. If we think of art in terms of an expressive problem to be solved, we can see how art experiences contribute to every field of human endeavor.

Children love art experiences. Whenever I have found a child who was not eager to participate in art activities, I have soon discovered an unfortunate situation in which some adult was too critical, made a disparaging remark or asked an abrupt question about the child's efforts. Although adults generally do not *mean* to discourage children, their senseless comments often stick with children long after the incident itself is forgotten. We have already considered the importance of sharing experiences with children. Now let us explore how we can provide basic materials and working space, and can encourage children to enjoy the process of discovery in using both.

## Basic Materials

Suitable art materials need not be expensive. Likewise, there is no need to start with everything at once. Although some people advocate providing a vast array of materials with the theory that if a child has enough materials he will create, I prefer a more moderate approach. We need to be concerned about the appropriateness of each material to the age level of the child. Some materials such as acrylic or oil paints could be used with a five- or six-year-old child, but, in my opinion, they are neither necessary nor practical. If younger children try every material, what is left to stimulate them later?

Recently, I saw an example of an oil painting done by a first grader whose mother is an artist. The painting was very small in format and more controlled in style than the large, bold tempera paintings typically done successfully by children of this age. Giving young children adult level materials fosters imitation of adult work and denies them the opportunity to discover painting techniques for themselves. The process of discovery is an essential criterion for development.

## Paper

The first materials provided for children should be crayons and paper. Large, plain paper with a non-shiny surface is desirable. Cream manila paper, colored construction paper, and newsprint paper may be purchased ready packaged. It is recommended that the standard 12 x 18 inch size be obtained. It is large enough to serve the young child's muscular development and can be cut down if necessary to fit specific needs. Because young children's larger muscles develop prior to the smaller finger muscles, their scribbles will cover a large area. For economy, one can substitute paper from store wrappings, grocery sacks, the back of wallpaper from sample books and rolls. The classified section of a newspaper, because of the even tone of the printing, can be used also. Sometimes the ends of newsprint rolls are available from newspaper or printing companies. The most important considerations are that the surface be as plain as possible and large enough to promote complete freedom. Often both sides can be used to save paper. Avoid giving the child ruled paper, typing paper or small scratch pads for they are neither suitable nor economical.

## Crayons

When purchasing crayons it is advisable to buy top quality ones because they provide greater economy in the long run as well as more effective color. Cheaper crayons contain more wax, are less brilliant and wear down faster. For the child's

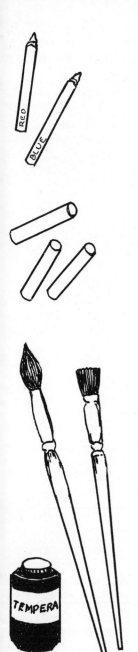

very first experience, the large size wax crayons in an eight-color assortment are quite adequate. Later, the standard size crayons in eight-color or sixteen-color sets are excellent. Children do not need elaborate assortments with many more colors per box. All crayons consist of coloring matter and a binder to hold them in stick form. All binders contain wax, but too much wax in cheaper crayons cause flaking problems in use and they may melt in the child's hand.

Crayons designated as "pressed" have less wax and more compression to create the stick. Pressed crayons are not recommended for young children because they require greater pressure making them more difficult to handle. As crayons are used, they are bound to get broken. Few commercial packages accommodate broken pieces, but short lengths offer highly creative alternatives to the pointed tip. Flat, sturdy boxes can be supplied to replace the original carton and will encourage diversity in use as well as encouragement to children to use them fully.

## Tempera paint

One of the most expressive materials for children to use is tempera paint. On many

occasions when adult observers visited my first grade classes, I found them amazed at the enthusiasm and skill of young children who were busily painting. A brush and liquid paint provide a direct and exciting medium which should never be curtailed by adult fears. Many children paint more freely and expressively than they draw with crayons. And above all, whether they are using crayons or paints, they should use them directly with *no previous pencil drawing*. Pencils and erasers have no place in the art expression of young children. Because there is no "right" or "wrong" way, there can be no mistakes. If this attitude is cultivated early, a child learns to change or modify as needed, without considering them mistakes. Adults who depend on pencils should avoid completely any sign of generating such fears in children.

Tempera paints can be purchased in liquid or powdered form, but the latter is far more economical. Liquid paints dry out if not covered tightly and are more costly initially. Although water can be added to keep liquid tempera paints moist, some colors become grainy if allowed to harden in the jar. Top quality powdered paint mixes instantly and does not deteriorate in the powdered form. When mixed, it lasts for considerable time if covered. Liquid tempera, also called poster paint or show card color, comes in several sizes. The smaller bottles often come in sets while larger size jars are usually sold separately. The one-pound container of powdered tempera, or powder paint, requires a greater initial expenditure but lasts considerably longer and extends the quantity when mixed. Small or large amounts can be mixed as needed.

A few suggestions can be offered to aid the effective use of tempera paints. Baby food jars or other jars with screw tops make good paint containers. Small plastic freezer cartons with lids also work well. Colors should be mixed to the consistency of heavy cream. For the very young child a few colors will suffice. Suggested colors are: red, yellow, blue, green, black and white. Desirable additions are: magenta, turquoise and brown. White is essential to give tints, for colors should not be "watered down" for lightness. Magenta and white make beautiful pinks; magenta and blue yield rich, brilliant violets. Turquoise and yellow expand the green range.

Tempera paints are opaque and should cover a surface readily. Children will discover that they mix on paper, when damp. If a color is dry, another hue may be painted on top without running if done very quickly. When tempera paints do not cover a surface (such as printing on a carton or newspaper surface) the addition of a small amount of white will usually help. Sometimes a small amount of liquid soap is added to improve covering and adhering qualities.

Papers listed as suitable for crayons may also be used with tempera paints. In addition, cardboard, corrugated board, carton and box sections and wrapping paper are suitable surfaces. Brushes should be easel type (bristle or soft hair) of a *large* size. If a child paints at an easel, a separate brush for each color is desirable but not essential. If a single brush is used, a container of water must be readily available. When a child paints at a table or on the floor, a sturdy wooden or cardboard box to hold the containers of mixed paint saves many a spill.

Another device to serve as a painting "palette" is a muffin tin. Considerable clean-up effort is saved if the waxed muffin liners are used for single colors can be removed without cleaning the entire tin. In any of the suggested paint containers, it is best to put only small amounts of each color of paint in each container, adding as needed. Children dislike using "dirty" paints caused by forgetting to wash the brush. Paints may be ready in screw-top jars from which small amounts are poured. A little ingenuity will soon create a practical method.

After children have learned how to work with crayons and paints, other materials may be added for variety. However, most children will continue to be challenged by crayon drawing and painting experiences so these basic art materials should always be available. Closely related to wax crayons are oil crayons or oil pastels. Both are used similarly on paper, but permit somewhat richer textural and color effects. Markers are popular with many children but it is very important that they be water-soluble, not permanent, type. In addition to the difficulty of removing marks from permanent markers, there is danger from breathing the fumes. Water-soluble markers in a range of hues come with various sized tips ranging from broad, felt tips to fine nylon tips. Because of their strong quality, markers encourage children to draw boldly and freely. Sometimes children enjoy combining them with other color media.

## Chalk

Colored chalk is an additional medium worthy of consideration. The chalk must be of the soft type intended for drawing, not the blackboard variety which is much harder. Sometimes the word "pastel" is used to designate a soft chalk suitable for children but should not be confused with artist's imported pastels. The qualities found in chalks which distinguish them from other media are velvety richness of brilliant color and ease of blending. Children enjoy them in spite of the fact that their softness makes them messy and difficult to keep without smearing. Any paper with sufficient "tooth" to permit chalk to adhere is needed. Smooth surfaces are not suitable for chalk. Manila and colored construction papers are excellent.

## Finger paint

Finger paint is another interesting material for children. The title is something of a misnomer for hands and arms are used as much as fingers in developing this medium to its full potential. A special coated paper sold where finger paints are stocked is essential. Some types of glazed shelf paper offer a substitute but not necessarily a saving in cost.

## Clay

Clay is also a valuable expressive medium. Some children respond more readily to a material that can be shaped or modeled three-dimensionally than to a material which is used two-dimensionally. Non-hardening, oil-based modeling clay can be purchased in various colors for the child to use over and over again. This type of clay should not be painted, but used in its natural state. Although water-based clay can be handled readily by a young child, it is more difficult to maintain at a workable consistency. If used, it can be painted when thoroughly dry with tempera paints. Objects treated thus can be recycled by washing off the paint, soaking the dry clay in water and reworking it to a proper consistency. Obviously this is more difficult and could be very discouraging to the young child.

Water-based clay is a natural product of the earth. When dug from local clay pits, it must be refined for best use. When purchased it has been blended and refined to meet the range of uses from pottery and ceramic wares to fine porcelain. Glazing and firing of clay are processes that should be delayed until later years. For the young child, emphasis should be placed on the modeling experience rather than the finished product. Self-hardening clays and those which may be baked in a kitchen oven should be avoided for they are very difficult to handle successfully.

## *Watercolors*

Watercolors, purchased in sets, are not recommended generally for children below the age of eight. Even for adults, the elusive quality of these transparent colors can be discouraging. After children have ample experience with opaque tempera paints, they may enjoy the boxed watercolors. If started at too early an age, they may be afraid to use them later. When children are ready and eager to have them, the eight color sets are suitable. Brushes should be large enough to hold ample supplies of paint yet capable of forming a point. Tiny brushes do not promote effective painting for children.

When purchasing crayons, tempera paints, chalks, watercolors, finger paints, modeling material, paste, and related art products, adults would be wise to watch for a small round seal with the letters CP. The Certified Products Bureau of the Crayon, Water Color and Craft Institute, Inc. of Orleans, Massachusetts, is a nationally-recognized association that regularly tests art materials. They give the CP Seal to those meeting standards certifying that the art product contains no materials in sufficient quantities to be toxic or injurious to the human body even if ingested.

The CP seal certifies quality as well as safety because CP products guarantee dependable materials for maximum creative expression.

The Crayon, Water Color and Craft Institute has worked with the National Bureau of Standards since 1943 in developing standards for children's art products. Because the National Bureau of Standards is no longer involved in this area, the Institute works directly with users and with the American National Standards Institute. It is also significant to note that the CP seal is recognized by the Poison Control Centers of the Public Health Service of the United States Government.

## Working Space

During children's preschool and early school years, it is essential that parents permit them to express themselves freely without specific directions or criticism. Educators have long recognized that the working process, the actual doing of art work, may be far more important and valuable to children than the product, the art work itself. Adults must restrain themselves from being critical of children who do not wish to save art work after they finish it or who fail to identify their own work at a later date. This is not to say that the product means nothing, but to caution against expecting a child to give it primary importance. The learning experience should be the major goal. As children produce more and more examples, they may begin to show pride in what they create, particularly if they sense adult approval of their efforts.

If we expect children to enjoy art experiences and to develop responsibility for continued activity, we must provide them with suitable working space. In warmer climates or during summer months, many art activities can be done successfully out-of-doors. In colder climates, it may be more desirable to create a suitable art area for children in a basement, attic, family room, utility room or in the child's own room. If possible, the area should be recognized specifically as an art area to be used and cared for by the child. Where space is limited, some form of portable work center can be created to be set up and cleared away at will. With very young children, adult supervision will be essential, but all efforts should be directed toward helping children assume responsibility step-by-step for this area. With the privilege of working must go the responsibility for care.

Let us consider how we might equip an art area for children. One of the first considerations is a washable floor covering such as linoleum, plastic, or cement. Some children prefer working directly on the floor. For many purposes a small table that fits the child's height plus a low, backless stool which may be pushed under the table when not in use will be most suitable. Painting easels are enjoyed by many young children. One can purchase single or double easels designed for children to work standing. They provide a painting surface large enough for paper 18 x 24 inches in size and an attached tray to hold several containers of paint. Many parents could construct either a standing or a table easel to accommodate their youngsters. Another helpful suggestion is the use of newspaper to protect working surfaces and to simplify clean-up. If children learn the habit of using newspapers to cover working areas at the outset, they will avoid many later problems. A small display area is a desirable addition. This will be discussed more fully later.

As soon as a working area is established, adults should help children devise suitable means of storage. If such an area is made attractive as well as practical, children can learn basic habits early in life. Both parents and children should learn to distinguish between a "working mess" evident when artwork is in progress and a "mess" left when materials are not cared for and put away after artwork is completed. There are countless ways to provide effective storage facilities. Small cartons, shoe boxes covered with wallpaper and stacked can form suitable shelving for many items. Ice cream buckets, plastic pails, shelves constructed from boards supported by bricks or glass blocks offer other possibilities. Plastic caddies used for household cleaning supplies may be purchased to carry supplies to a working location. Children should be encouraged to share in the planning as well as in continuous care.

No material, in itself, automatically guarantees that art will result. Children should be encouraged to explore possibilities for using scrap materials, discarded industrial materials, wood scraps, plus all kinds of collectible natural items. Unless some system is devised for sorting out and storing various items, the accumulation can become an overwhelming mess. Scraps of fabric or paper, yarns, string, buttons, other relatively flat objects can be used effectively in two-dimensional designs or collages. Wood scraps, other waste material can become exciting three-dimensional constructions or mobiles. In order to utilize these items fully, children will need to have additional supplies available: scissors, paste, white glue (washable), stapler, and possibly hammer and nails or tacks. Wire is generally not recommended because it is potentially dangerous unless handled with very great care.

We have already stressed the importance of permitting children complete freedom of expression, meaning that adults should not tell them specifically *what* to make or exactly *how* to express it. We need to be aware, however, of certain procedural steps that can stimulate children to be successful instead of becoming frustrated in their efforts. For example, adults need to help children know how to care for their brushes. After each use, a brush used in tempera or watercolor should be washed thoroughly with water, and occasionally with soap, and reshaped to its original form. If a brush is capable of forming a point, it should be gently shaped and allowed to dry. A wedge-shaped tip should be left in that condition to dry. Brushes should never be left standing in paint, should not be twisted or scrubbed. With care, brushes last a long time and give effective service.

Another example can be noted in the case of finger painting. For best results, the glazed paper must be rolled and dipped in water, unrolled and spread with the glazed side up on a water-resistant tabletop, smoothed by the palm of the hand or a sponge to remove air bubbles, and it is ready to be used. A small amount of finger paint is spread across the wet surface and manipulated with hand, arm and fingers. It may be reworked as long as the surface remains moist, but too much redoing may wear through the paper. Obviously, adults can help children learn how to set up their materials, but after that, the children must decide how to develop their own ideas. Once or twice showing the procedures should enable children to repeat the process for themselves. Often older children can assist younger ones. Other examples of procedural hints will be provided later.

Many times it is desirable for children and adults to share in the process of discovery, but the adults should not dominate. As soon as children show that they are able to continue, the adult should hold back. We cannot assume automatically that adults will produce superior results for, in fact, the reverse may be the case. If adults can learn graciously from children so that true sharing occurs, all can profit. But as soon as adults feel self-conscious about their efforts, they should leave the expression to the children. Again, we repeat that adults play their most important role when they provide the experiences, the facilities and the encouragement to enable children to express themselves freely.

Throughout this entire process it should be evident that all patterns, copying, coloring books and other stereotyped devices should be completely avoided. Unfortunately, commercialization of such items has made them so readily available that adults buy them without realizing how much harm they do to children. Research has proven conclusively that the cliché of "learning to color inside the lines" is a false and damaging objective. Commercially produced devices are "crutches" which deprive children of gaining the power to think for themselves. Learning to make choices, to exercise their expressive powers, to act independently are all steps that help children to become responsible adults.

I recall an incident a mother related to me about her three children's experience with coloring books. The three boys, ages six, seven, and eight, always played together, and whenever all three appeared before their mother, she knew she must take time to listen. On this occasion, the eight-year-old spoke for all three when he asked her, "Mother, how much longer do we have to use these *stupid* coloring books?" Although taken somewhat by surprise, she quickly responded by asking, "What would you like instead?" Very quickly they asked for big sheets of plain paper and crayons. She concluded the incident by relating that they had been "going to town" on their own ideas ever since. Unfortunately, not all children are capable of identifying the problem or have sufficient rapport with adults to request a change. If adults doubt these boys' apt description of "stupid" coloring books, then they should take time to discover the trite, outdated items regularly included. Children usually create far more distinctively personal forms of expression than those found in most commercial aids.

We have stressed continuously the significance of self-discovery on the part of children to enable them to enhance their own self-image and begin to exercise their capacities to think independently. By the time children have experienced considerable opportunity for self-expression, we can begin to develop their consciousness of basic elements and principles of art which are universally recognized. In the next chapter we shall look at ways we can involve them in this direction.

# 4

# Giving Meaning
# to Art Expression

ANYONE WHO HAS BEEN AROUND YOUNG CHILDREN knows how quickly they add new words to their vocabularies. It also becomes evident very soon that if we do not encourage them to learn and understand terms that challenge their thinking, they may surprise us with words we prefer not to hear.

Certain terms basic to the language of art are widely accepted wherever art expression is evident. Educators believe that these universal concepts can be taught at any age provided they are approached on the level of the learner. This means that adults should know and use the basic language of art consistently with young children without trying to substitute simpler terms. At the same time, they need to discover descriptive words and phrases within the vocabulary range of young children as they define the terms and build experiences that make them visually understandable. The process can be an exciting learning experience for both adults and children.

What are the basic art terms employed universally throughout every person's life span? We are referring to the *elements* and *principles* of *design* which are employed to create the *composition* of works of art. Many of the terms can be found in other arts as well. For example, the principle of *rhythm* is found in visual arts such as painting, but also is observed in music, in poetry, in dance. We speak of a composer creating a musical composition, but we know also that a writer composes a novel, a poem, a play, a choreographer composes a series of movements to create a dance composition, or an architect creates the structural composition or plan for a building.

Every term is common in daily usage but needs to be defined more specifically in relation to visual arts. For young children, each term requires more than verbal use through words alone. Each needs to be observed in a multitude of situations and then explored through experiments with art materials and processes. As children grow, their exploration can be extended and deepened to increase the meaningfulness of the basic concepts. The concepts themselves do not change.

What are the basic *elements* of design? Generally we name *line, form, space, color,* and *texture* as the five universal elements employed in art expression. Likewise, *balance, rhythm,* and *emphasis* constitute the three accepted *principles* of design. It should be readily apparent that these are not strange words, for all can be employed readily in the context of our daily conversation. We know also that children can learn to say and use these words very early in life even though they may not learn to spell them or write them until later. We need, then, to discover how we can make each term function effectively in children's experiences.

Again, we must point out the importance of adults sharing with children the many observational aspects relating to the basic elements and principles of design. As we consider each one individually we will suggest ways for adults to introduce each concept to children, examples of situations where adults and children together can observe each concept, follow-up experiences, games and activities children can pursue with guidance or on their own with adult interest and support, and possible art exploration of each. Our suggestions will not always retain a specific order because, after the introduction and observation, a child will continue to see new examples that will reinforce the continuity of experience. Simple games can often challenge further exploration. Many times children will devise their own continuing experiences, building new activities upon former ones. The learning process can be endless if sufficient encouragement and acceptance from adults are present.

## Searching for Lines

Line is often described as the path our vision takes. Line is essentially a human concept; it is the reaction of our eyes to a given visual stimulus. We see *straight* lines repeated in a picket fence, in rails and ties of a railroad track, the *edges* of doors, windows, sidewalks, bricks, blocks, furniture, pieces of paper, and in countless other places. We observe *curved* lines in the *edges* of leaves, in branches and bushes, in parts of our bodies, in fruits and vegetables, in arches, and in numerous other examples. We quickly associate *wavy* lines with water and *zigzag* lines with lightning. We can define each further by noting if lines are long or short, thick or thin, heavy or light.

The first step necessary is to help children identify and name the various kinds of line—straight, curved, wavy, zigzag—by observing them, wherever convenient, and talking about them. Our home, our community, and nature itself provide endless resources for observing lines. Because children enjoy games, we can devise simple game activities to stimulate more intensive observation. Where more than one child is present, it is easy to stimulate them to see who can find a different example. However, the natural competitive spirit should be respected without resorting to rewards or prizes.

After observing the diverse qualities of lines in our surroundings, the next step may be to discover how line is used to enhance objects as differentiated from the way line defines the structure of an object. In this category we see the lines dividing a window into smaller patterns instead of the lines outlining the shape of the frame; we discover the use of lines creating

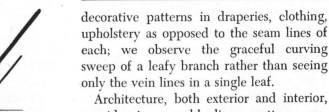

decorative patterns in draperies, clothing, upholstery as opposed to the seam lines of each; we observe the graceful curving sweep of a leafy branch rather than seeing only the vein lines in a single leaf.

Architecture, both exterior and interior, provides innumerable linear patterns created to make structures more appealing visually—brick, stone, and block patterns; floor surface designs; decorative railings; wallpaper; windows, organ pipes, and other details in churches; windows in schools, stores, factories; graphics; pipes, chimneys, electrical fixtures; and others too numerous to mention. All we need to do is sit or stand in one spot for five minutes and note the diversity of lines that we are often too preoccupied to notice, to realize how easily we can cultivate the observational powers of children.

Because line is one of the simplest elements to observe, we can readily stimulate this activity with young children. After we have shared many initial experiences and discussed them with children, we can challenge them to find other examples in their surroundings. Because they are not able to write down what they find, we need to take time out for them to show us what they discover. For example, suppose a mother is busy baking and needs to be undisturbed. She might suggest to her little boy or girl that he or she go to a designated part of the house to look for examples of long, thin lines, or curved lines, or some other specific kind. She will tell her child that as soon as she puts the baking in the oven, she will come to see what that child has found. As a variation, the child might use crayon and paper to draw the examples, then explain each. A caution is necessary that we must accept the explanation rather than seek quality in the drawing itself, for the real purpose of the exercise is observation. But we must take time to listen. Older and younger children in the same household can be encouraged to devise their own games of this nature, reporting to one another, as well as to parents.

Children who have been stimulated to observe lines of every sort can be encouraged to express themselves through the use of line. In many cases, children who have space and materials available will initiate their own expression. It should be noted that by suggesting certain limits, we do not restrict the child's creativity, but rather we challenge greater inventiveness. Too much freedom can be overwhelming and counterproductive. Poster paint, crayons (both tip and flat side), chalk, and paper are materials which can be used effectively.

Try the following suggestions as starters, then devise others to encourage children to expand their own expression:

- Paint a striped design using only one color for thick, straight lines and another color for thin straight lines. Repeat using curving, wavy, or zigzag lines.

- Make a striped or plaid design using both crayon tips and the flat side of short pieces to produce varied quality lines.

- Arrange paper strips in a pattern. Paste the strips when you like your design.

## Identifying Form

We have observed that line frequently is observed as the *edge* of an object. The area thus defined becomes the *form* or *shape* of the space that is enclosed visually. Although we often use the words shape and form interchangeably, we speak more accurately of flat, two-dimensional shapes and massive three-dimensional forms.

What are some of the *shapes* children can identify readily? Circles, triangles, squares and rectangles are the most common ones to be observed, but children can also learn about ovals, stars, free-formed shapes, and even many-sided figures such as hexagons or octagons. As in the case of lines, it does not take much effort to observe shapes all around us. The lines close to become shapes.

Innumerable *circles* can be discovered in dishes, glassware, kitchen utensils, wheels, tires, machinery parts, flowers, lampshades, toys, games, clocks, dials, and in other objects. *Triangles* can be found in the gables of houses, sails, traffic signs, banners and flags, for example. *Squares* and *rectangles* will be revealed in architectural details such as doors, windows, floor tiles, bricks, blocks, pictures, mirrors, rugs, paving sections, newspaper and magazine shapes, to name a few. Free-formed shapes can be observed in nature in flower beds, shapes of ponds or lakes, as well as in household objects.

When we add depth to common shapes, we recognize *forms* such as the sphere, cone, pyramid, cube, and rectangular blocks. Children's toys and blocks will provide familiar examples as a starting point. Added observation in the environment will expand their familiarity with these basic forms.

Because line, shape, and form are so closely related, exploration of these concepts can often be carried out simultaneously. For example, after identifying straight line edges, it is a natural step to observe that when we combine four equal length lines and four corners we have a square. Add depth, and the square becomes a cube. In continuing, if the four sides of a square form a base and each edge of that square becomes one side of a triangle, we can create a pyramid. We can do much to enhance children's learning if we help them experience excitement through such discoveries.

Parents can devise various game experiences to involve chil-

dren in learning about shapes and forms. These can range from simple sorting and matching of precut shapes to searching for examples in their own home, in nature, in magazine illustrations or in other situations. Art expression with paints, crayons, cut paper can follow similar directions as suggested under the exploration of various lines, using repeated shapes of varying sizes in designs.

In addition, try out the following examples:

- Choose *one* large (10 or 12 inches) shape—a circle, square, rectangle, or triangle. Fold the chosen shape in half, cutting from the folded edge as many successive duplicate shapes as possible with no waste.

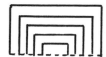
*fold*

Unfold the hollow squares (or other shapes) and arrange in an overlapping design. Paste design on a sheet of paper of another color.

- Repeat the process using two different shapes, each of a separate color.
- Construct a three-dimensional structure from boxes, paper tubes, other forms.

## Exploring Space

For very young children, the concept of *space* is dominantly physical. They move about in defined spatial areas at home, in their community and beyond. Space is identified by their various activities. Gradually, space begins to assume other meanings such as the area inside a shape, around a shape or between shapes. Undoubtedly, understanding of space to many children will be felt more than seen because their activities will occur within a circumscribed area or space—a room in their home, their yard, the school, the church, the park, the playground, or in a play space of their own devising. Many children can be observed creating their own play space from cartons, pieces of furniture, blocks, other objects which in their imaginations can be anything from a castle to a space ship.

Many children have gained considerable knowledge of areas beyond their immediate personal contacts through television. Whether they play they are in a remote part of the world or traversing outer space, they create their own feeling for space and operate as though they are there in reality.

Parents can enhance children's visualization of space concepts by helping them to observe the variations in range of spatial aspects, such as: near and far, big and little, inside and outside, above and below, in and out, open and closed. Many of these ideas can be readily observable in nature and adults can stimulate children's thinking whether they are enjoying vast landscapes of woods, hills, mountains, lakes, deserts, or simply looking at things in the backyard. Discussing what is seen together increases understanding and feeling.

In any art expression, children create within a given space. If they are working on a sheet of paper, they should be encouraged to "fill the space" as effectively as possible. Instead of drawing or painting one item in the middle of the page, children can be given suggestions to use the entire sheet. Along with this idea, we can help children become conscious of creating something important to see, or of having a "center of interest." The latter is equally important in three-dimensional compositions and can often be observed by asking, "What do you see first?" Sometimes we can state it by saying, "What is it that you want *me* to notice?" Suggestions can be offered of ways to make the important "center of interest" more pleasing. However, adults can encourage children to think of things to add or change, but they must let children make their own choices and decisions.

In order to stimulate consciousness of space, children can be encouraged to construct various forms in space. Two types of construction experiences can be particularly meaningful:

- Construction in sand, either at the beach, along a river bank or in a sand box helps children sense space concepts in miniature form.

- Creation of a play area can be encouraged if parents help children obtain large cartons, other materials from which they can create imaginary places.

## Relating Colors

Color is one of the most pervasive elements in visual arts. With the exception of sculpture which depends more on form, and some types of print making which rely on black/white contrast for effectiveness, most visual arts capitalize on color. Most adults tend to use the word "color" all-inclusively because they are unaware of more definitive terms. We can make our appreciation and use of color more effective if we distinguish among three aspects or dimensions of color.

The first term we need to use more frequently is *hue*, which is simply the name of the specific color. The names we use should be the basic ones: red, orange, yellow, green, blue, violet, brown, black, white. We should avoid popular names which change with fads and seasons, such as: Alice blue, apple green, luggage tan, burnt orange, hot pink, mahogany, burgundy, others. As children's color experiences increase, they will discover for themselves that there are gradations of hues and will begin to recognize that red-violet lies between red and violet, and other such combinations. Gradually they will acquire hue names which have gained common identification such as turquoise and magenta.

The second important term is *brightness* or *value* and denotes a range or scale. When we discover that some hues are lighter, some are darker than others, we are recognizing that a range exists. The nearer a hue is to white, the lighter it is or the higher it is on the scale of brightness or value. The closer a hue is to black, the darker or lower it lies on the scale. We describe these variations typically by speaking of "light to dark" or "tint to shade."

Generally speaking, children's earliest efforts with color will be characterized by pure hues in paint or crayon. As they accidentally happen to get more water in a particular hue in their painting, their blue may become light blue for the first time or they observe other similar tints. Likewise, as soon as children add white paint, they discover the excitement of red becoming pink or similar hue variations. Subsequent "accidents" with various hues account for color discoveries that stimulate the kind of learning words alone cannot accomplish.

The third dimension of color, *saturation* or *intensity*, further delineates a specific hue by describing how red, how blue or how green it is. We can also speak of the redness, blueness or greenness. As already noted, children frequently choose strong, pure hues in their work. Adults can accurately describe such pure color as "intense" or "highly saturated," but children will continue to utilize such hues in their work naturally long before they acquire the appropriate terminology. Less intense or duller hues are not apt to be the first choices of most children and their appreciation of greyed tones will occur much later.

Early in my teaching I followed an art teacher who had been in the same school for over twenty years. I was appalled to discover in the paper storage cabinet that there were huge stacks of colored construction paper in violets, greyed greens, dull blues, tans, pale yellows, but virtually no pure reds, yellows, blues, greens. These papers were so old that they were faded at the edges and so brittle they cracked when folded. Her adult taste for subtle, greyed hues was obviously not shared by the children. The same thing can be noted if one looks at the crayons which are left after a few weeks of use. Reds, blues, greens, and blacks will be worn down to tiny stubs while others may still retain their pointed tips.

Many adults, at some time in their experience, have been taught a "color wheel" and perhaps "standard color harmonies." These have no place in the education of young children and dubious value for anyone if treated as formal rules only. The most vital concept which influences our total understanding of color is that "all color is relative." Color is never viewed in isolation but is always seen in relationship to other hues. Whenever we try to observe a particular hue, we must note what other hues are present to affect it and whether we see it in full light or in shadow, for its appearance is never constant.

Observing these ever-changing relationships can become a fascinating process to adults who have never discovered color relationships through a visual process. Children will benefit from guidance in discovering color phenomena through continuous experiences beginning with the simplest aspects and moving to more complex considerations only as they are mature enough to grasp them. Only after children discover various color phenomena through personal experience should the appropriate terms be introduced. The field of color knowledge is too vast even for scientists to have all the answers. But every human being is affected daily by color relationships and can benefit greatly by developing an open, inquiring mind from earliest childhood to maturity.

In developing the following color experiences, adults are urged to participate directly with children, discussing various aspects throughout the entire process. Each suggestion may be treated as a color game for all involved.

- Discover *color families* by looking around a room or given area for as many examples as possible of red, of yellow, and of blue. If more than one child is present, each child might search for examples of a single hue. Were there any items that seemed to fit more than one hue? For example, was it difficult to decide whether an orange item belonged in the red or yellow family? If so, a color mixing experience might follow effectively.

- *Hue variations* can be discovered in another type of experience. Each participant should choose a single hue, such as red, and assemble as many samples as possible from various art materials (crayon, paint, chalk, paper), from magazine pages, from fabrics, or other sources. Which ones are similar? Which are different? Does texture modify the hue?

- *Hue variations* in nature can be exciting to discover. For example, look for variations in green and discuss the similarities and differences.

- Arranging samples of a single hue, such as blue, from the highest (nearness to white) to the lowest (nearness to black) will help children discover the *brightness levels* or *value scale*. Discuss where you might find each blue — sky, water, clothing, other places.

- *Color mixing* which may have occurred by accident sets the stage for some revealing exercises.

Paint mixing is one way to discover how secondary colors are created from primary colors: red plus yellow makes orange, yellow plus blue makes green, and blue plus red makes violet. As children get older, they will begin to discover even finer gradations such as yellow-orange, blue-green, red-violet, others.

- *Color modification* can be revealed through a simple test that may be more meaningful as the child gets a little older. From eight basic hues (red, orange, yellow, green, blue, violet, brown, black) of crayons, choose *one*, such as yellow. On a sheet of manila paper, color eight patches approximately two inches square. Leave one patch the original hue and color *across* each of the remaining seven with one of the other hues. After completing all eight samples, look around the house and out of doors to find objects which approximate the new hues. Children will discover a mixture which looks like brick, another may look like weathered wood, a plant, some other object. Such observation is valuable and children will become more discerning in time even though they may continue to draw and paint using "pure" hues.

All color experiences should be regarded as ways to stimulate the observational powers of children, not as directives. Young children use color intuitively and approach art openly and freely. Adults need to use extreme caution lest they destroy the charming quality of children's unique personal expression. Emphasis should be placed on discovery of exciting color experiences without dictating or influencing children's art expression directly.

## Sensing Textures

Of all the elements of design, texture relates more to our sense of touch than to sight alone. However, in its most sophisticated aspects, visual textural effects can literally fool our eyes. Over the ages, artists have employed tromp-l'oeil effects so cleverly to "fool the eye" that the viewer tries to brush off the fly realistically perched on an object in the painting. With the development of photography artists have no real need to recreate nature, but they try to stimulate the viewer to feel nature more intensely. Texture can become a vital aspect linking closely to color in the art expression of children.

Try rubbing your hand across a marble table top, a highly polished wooden surface, a mirror, a brick or stone wall, a cement sidewalk, a window screen, the bark of a tree, freshly mowed grass, a piece of sandpaper. Feel fur, velvet, tweed, burlap, satin fabrics, or walk barefoot across carpeting, sand, gravel, or touch other surfaces. How did each one feel? Could you describe the texture of each? Did words such as smooth, silky, rough, grainy, soft, scratchy, hard come to mind? Children will soon learn to describe their reactions in more descriptive terms than hard and soft, rough and smooth, provided their experiences help to increase their awareness of diverse textures.

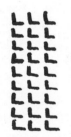

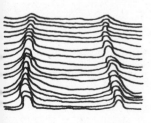

Texture can be *actual;* that is, it can really exist on the surface. Children and artists alike create surface textures in

their work. Clay can be rough or smooth according to the way the surface is handled. Varied textures in paper, fabrics, even paint quality are employed to enhance the feeling quality. Our eyes sense such variations even when we do not actually touch the surface.

*Simulated* textures offer alternative approaches which create similar reactions in viewers. The appearance of roughness can be accomplished by varied repetitions of lines, patterns, and shapes. Magazine advertising is a familiar example of simulated textural effects which fool our eyes consistently. Just as children demonstrate a natural sense of color, so they often employ surface patterns in their work intuitively and charmingly. When we offer them new ways to sense texture through exercises, we may enable them to become more adventurous and creative in subsequent art expression. Again, the exercises we stimulate will not necessarily result directly in art production, but should help to create greater awareness. The following suggestions focus on texture:

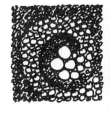

- Assemble a group of items inside a large paper sack, selecting each for its textural variation. Play a game in which a child feels objects one by one, without looking, and describes how each feels.

- Make rubbings by placing thin paper, such as newsprint, over various surfaces, rubbing over the surface with the broad side

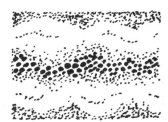

of a piece of crayon to transfer the surface texture to the paper. Talk about the variations discovered.

- Press or roll out a flat slab of clay. Create texture with fingers or by impressing various objects into the clay. This can be redone frequently to discover new ways rather than thinking of it as an art product.

- Create textural patterns in sand at the beach, along the river bank, or in a sand box. Add sticks, stones, shells, or other available items to enhance both the form and the surface texture.

## Creating Balance

Almost everyone who has played on a teeter-totter has learned how to compensate when the two persons are of unequal weights. The simple shifting of the board to give the lighter person the longer end is the same principle involved in achieving visual balance. Objects in artistic compositions do not have to be identical to appear balanced. Size, color, and position can all affect visual weight.

As we observe children's art expression, we note that they achieve balance in seemingly nonconventional ways. Because their sense of formal perspective is undeveloped, they do not employ usual ways of showing distance, but create a remarkable effect of balanced space through very direct, simple methods. We should never attempt to force conformity but should bend our efforts toward developing their observation of and feeling for balance. Their natural expression will follow accordingly.

The most obvious form of balance, achieved when like objects are placed on either side of center, is called *formal* balance. If we again refer to the teeter-totter, we would have children of equal size placed on equal ends of the board, but they might not be identical twins. Where do we observe formal balance in our daily experience? We see it in architecture—in buildings, houses, synagogues, and churches having a central entrance doorway and windows of identical size and placement on either side. We observe it in clothing—in dresses, jackets, blouses, shirts, sweaters which have identical sides. We create it when we fold a paper in half, cut a design, and open it to reveal both halves alike.

Formal balance is always more obvious, and for that reason, is not preferred in many situations. The more subtle and comfortable type is referred to as *informal* balance. We need to be aware of the fact that informal balance is equally balanced but is achieved in ways many find more appealing. We must not confuse it with imbalance or consider it out-of-balance, for informal balance requires highly sensitive feelings to achieve the finest results. Generally, we can again apply the teeter-totter principle when we observe visual balance of unlike objects. The object which is larger or stronger in color and visual dominance is placed closer to the imaginary center of the composition and the less prominent ones are placed farther away to balance the larger form. Often one more dominant object will be balanced by several smaller items.

We can observe beautiful examples of informal balance in architecture which utilizes diverse shapes, places doors at corners or away from center, and uses windows in varied patterns. We see it in interior arrangements of furniture stressing uneven placement of groups. We see it in gardens, flower arrangement, clothing, paintings, sculpture, fabric patterns, and in countless other places in everyday life. The Japanese are noted for their subtle arrangements utilizing informal balance.

The third type of balance is called *radial* balance, taking its name from the radiating spokes of a wheel. We can easily think of wheels on everything from automobiles, bicycles, wagons, clock faces, the sun, dials to the wheels connected with implements like hand drills, eggbeaters and such. Flowers like daisies with their radiating petals offer other examples. Not to be overlooked are the great rose windows of many churches.

In a closely related aspect, we can observe the semicircular or fan-shaped forms found in the peacock's tail, in fan windows over doorways, fireplace screens, and in many other examples.

Children can be stimulated to explore physical balance in other ways than playing on the teeter-totter. As they play with blocks and toys, they will have numerous opportunities to discover that objects tip over unless properly balanced. They can be guided in finding the point at which a stick, a pencil, a rod, a ruler will balance when held across one finger. Mobiles are great art forms to observe, for they combine balance and movement in ever-changing patterns.

Even young children can enjoy helping with simple tasks at home that involve balance. Helping set the table requires balance of utensils at each place. Arranging bouquets of garden flowers, greens, or dried plants call for discrimination in balancing various colors and shapes which children soon learn if parents are patient throughout the learning process. Arranging for display of their own artwork requires sensitivity to balance. These are but a few examples offering daily opportunities for children to participate in continuous learning and awareness.

I recall from my own childhood that I thoroughly enjoyed folding paper to cut patterns. One of my long-time favorites was cutting snowflakes of all sizes from those about nine inches in diameter to tiny ones only a couple of inches across. Once children learn to fold the paper correctly, they can achieve beautiful six-sided snowflakes again and again. As with other suggestions, adults should give only enough guidance to stimulate the process. The children should choose for themselves.

A few ideas may encourage further exploration:

- Show children how to fold paper in half, cutting *away* from the fold, so that a symmetrical shape is achieved when opened. Among the earliest forms cut by children are Valentine hearts, evergreen trees and bells for the Christmas season. However, we should never ridicule the simple lop-sided hearts, trees or other forms children cut as long as they satisfy their need for expression. By watching and listening, but not forcing, adults can sense when children require more advanced methods. We can show them the process, but we must insist that they make their own. We must not do it for them.

- A follow-up of a single-cut form is to use repeated folds in one direction to cut multiple shapes strung together. This will be more suitable for slightly older children.
- Fold paper to cut snowflakes. *Thin* paper is necessary to keep folds from becoming too heavy to cut. (See Art Processes Guide.)
- Create a wood construction from small scrap pieces which can stand alone.

## Sensing Rhythm

Young children have a remarkable natural sense of movement or rhythm. As they develop physically, their bodies respond readily to music, to games with balls, to jumping rope, and other forms of movement. Because life itself possesses rhythmic patterns—heart heat, breathing, eating, sleeping, to name a few examples—it is natural to feel rhythm constantly. Besides being actively involved in rhythmic movement, people learn to appreciate those aspects which come largely through our senses of sight and hearing. We can listen to music and feel its rhythm without necessarily dancing or making overt movements. Likewise, we can sense rhythmic patterns visually and become conscious of them in visual arts and learn to employ the principles in our own expression.

Much of the art expression of children, from the first scribbles, involves distinctly kinesthetic activity. The processes of drawing, painting, modeling, others all involve definite physical activity and will be internalized by children before they are able to analyze them verbally. When children become deeply engrossed in an art process, they often accompany their art activity with appropriate sounds or movements.

Certain concepts related to the principle of rhythm are useful in observing and analyzing visual effects. *Continuity* is a vital element that may be observed in the rhythmic line created by a skater performing on ice, in the tracks made by a skier in fresh snow, by an animal's tracks through the woods, by the path a worm creates in the garden, and in other similar situations. Continuity of line is observable in numerous forms of visual arts as well as in music, dance, and other arts.

*Repetition* is a key element which can be observed again and again. Helping children observe repetition in nature can not only occupy them constructively but can also stimulate their own expressive acts. We can listen to the repetitious patterns in the songs of birds, the hum of insects, the sounds made by animals. We see repetition in leaf, flower, tree shapes. We can feel it in gusts of wind, waves beating along the beach, in the drops of rain. We feel rhythmic repetition of drum beats, of dancers' steps, of the take-off roar of airplanes, the barking of a dog, of words. We hear and learn the oft-repeated words associated with hymns and religious rituals. The examples are endless for repetition is a part of every aspect of daily life.

Likewise, we can observe the repetition of lines, shapes, colors and textures in the visual arts. Repetition of lines and shapes can be instrumental in stimulating texture in various art forms. In developing a painting, an artist deliberately repeats elements such as line, shape, color or texture to develop unity in the composition or to call attention by accenting certain details. Discovering uses of repetition can be a long-time continuous process for the variations are endless.

The third aspect of rhythm to be noted is *progression* of visual elements: from small to large shapes, from light to dark color, from thick to thin lines. The field of advertising makes frequent use of progression to lead the eye of the viewer to the product being advertised. The use of progression creates a very dramatic effect and is found in various arts involving sound, as from soft to loud, from melodic to dissonant. Color progression from light to dark or from tint to shade has already been noted. Children playing with blocks or other construction toys will often be observed arranging or stacking them in order of size. They respond to a natural feeling for sequential order.

In addition to developing a sense of rhythm, children can be stimulated to search for or create their own examples. These suggestions may lead to others:

- Create a pattern by folding paper into smaller block units and repeating the *same unit design in* each space. A more advanced process involves alternations of two design units. Fabric, wallpaper and gift wrapping paper patterns utilize such repeated designs. Children can create their own gift wrapping papers in this manner.

- Use a series of like shapes ranging in size from small to large to create a dynamic design using progression.

- Look for examples of progression in magazine advertisements.

- Collect small sticks or twigs and arrange them in a repeated line design.

## Observing Emphasis

Have you ever analyzed your own speech with children to discover what things you stress? Undoubtedly, you emphasize certain admonitions, scoldings, or directions frequently. Do you place equal emphasis upon words indicating pleasurable reactions to children's efforts? *Emphasis* is such a common part of our daily conversation that it may be difficult to transfer the concept to its positive aspects in relation to visual art. We have previously noted the importance of the "center of interest" in children's art work under our discussion of the element of space. It is also a matter of emphasis because *contrast* is important in projecting visual ideas.

Children will usually give greater importance to the most significant aspect of their art expression naturally, but there are ways to help them become more conscious of the principle in art. Often it is a matter of asking a child, "What is the most important part of your picture?" Or in looking at a child's efforts, we could hold it a little distance away and say to the child, "Does it show as much as you want it to show?" If he is not satisfied, we can continue to see how it can be made more emphatic by making suggestions.

What are the most common ways to emphasize? We know quickly that color relationships are crucial with the most dominant color reserved for the most important part. At times, a distinctive shape will stand out from more ordinary ones. Powerful lines can lead the eye in the desired direction or space may be used to set off an object. Along with color, texture assumes importance in distinguishing specific aspects. In other words, all the elements contribute toward generating the desired emphasis. Experiments suggested under various elements and principles can serve to increase awareness of emphasis.

It should be obvious to adults who have followed this discussion of the elements and principles of art that there is considerable overlapping, and that there are many ways to build appropriate understanding. In practice we employ them together but it is useful to try to separate them in order to generate a richer understanding of each. Through sharing experiences adults and children are more able to increase their mutual respect. If adults and children learn together to understand and appreciate the wonders of God's universe, they should also become more sensitive to the needs of other human beings everywhere in the world. Art expression provides an undeniably sensitive approach.

# 5

# Putting It All Together

LEARNING IS EXCITING, PARTICULARLY FOR CHILDREN. Each day in their young lives brings new ideas to stimulate their imaginations. Things that seem ordinary to adults present challenges that have no bounds to young learners. For adults to have a part in sharing means a new way of looking at the day-to-day experiences through the eyes of children thereby gaining a new sense of the meaning of life.

We have already looked at the great variety of experiences that adults can share with children. We have considered the kinds of art materials and working space appropriate for young children. And we have examined the basic elements and principles underlying all art. But if we wish to help children progress in their artistic expression, we must consider more carefully how we weave all these concepts into a working unity that can continue throughout life. Because much of any individual's behavior is formed during the early years, we must encourage our children to develop as fully as possible during childhood.

Currently there is much more general recognition of the fact that human beings need *both* visual and verbal skills throughout life. Reference was made in Chapter 1 to the development of the right and left hemispheres of the brain. Many believe that this development must occur in complementary fashion with each strengthening the other to create balance. It might be said in recognition of the visual world in which we exist that human beings must think visually and see thoughtfully in order to function completely. The purpose of seeing is to arouse the mind to creative activity. How can adults facilitate this process?

First let us consider the elements which are involved when children engage in creative activities. Although the sequence may vary, the following aspects are related to the expressive process:

- idea or theme derived from personal observation or experience
- choice of materials or medium of expression
- selection of process or method of handling media
- utilization of basic elements and principles of art
- sharing and enjoying creative effort

Although children may be stimulated temporarily by an unfamiliar material or process, these considerations are generally subordinated to the idea or theme to be expressed. If we assume that children have already explored materials and processes to discover for themselves what each can do, our attention then focuses primarily on the stimulation of ideas that occurs as the result of both extensive and intensive observation and experience in the world around them. Let us examine the facets of a child's world from which ideas may be generated.

The *human world* encompasses those persons, activities and qualities which impinge upon children from birth onward influencing every phase of their lives. Included are:

- the self, family, relatives
- friends, playmates, neighbors

- professional people — doctor, dentist, nurse, police, teachers, clergy
- workers—grocer, mail carrier, clerks, telephone operator, mechanic, factory worker, truck driver, construction worker, farmer, others
- people of other races, creeds, countries
- people-centered activities
- emotional atmosphere, feeling tone generated in human relationships

The *natural world* takes into consideration all aspects of the physical environment, which relate to children's experiences:

- plants, trees, flowers, farms, gardens
- rivers, streams, lakes, oceans
- animals, birds, insects, fish, undersea life
- forests, hills, mountains, plains, deserts
- sun, moon, stars, planets, heavens
- wind, rain, snow, sleet, hail, storms

The *fabricated world* deals with all places and objects constructed by people to enhance their living, namely:

- homes, furniture, appliances, television, radio
- churches, schools, public buildings, libraries, theaters
- stores, factories, malls, shopping centers
- towns, cities
- transportation — cars, trucks, trains, buses, airplanes, recreational vehicles
- hospitals, clinics, offices
- museums, art galleries, concert halls
- playgrounds, parks, recreation centers

The *imaginary world* deals with those deeply personal elements dear to the hearts of children which are typified by:

- dreams
- books, stories, poems, plays
- wishes

The *spiritual world,* though somewhat more nebulous to define, exerts great influence upon the lives of children. Examples are:

- love of God
- respect for other human beings
- feeling of self-worth
- loyalty and commitment to others
- trust
- wonder in the universe

## Giving Significance to Expression

### Picture Making and Design Activities

Many young children, when provided with art materials and working space, will draw and paint, expressing their ideas freely. Picture making will generally constitute the most prevalent form of expression. However, without stimulation and encouragement, their illustrations may become repetitive and sterile showing little development. Because people play such an important role in their lives, they will draw or paint them readily showing full figure, head only, from waist up, and generally in frontal rather than profile view. Their earliest efforts will reveal little concern for proportion, details or logical placement of body parts. Gradually they will begin to show action and add appropriate details. Observation of significant details should be encouraged when appropriate to children's expressive purposes, but not as correction of their modes of expression.

As children identify with *who* in their expression, they can be encouraged to add *what, where, how* and *why.* Conversation to extend the child's *own* thinking is valuable, but should not be used to force adult ideas or to correct the child's intent. After the who-what action is established, children can be encouraged by expanding their observation of the natural environment, the fabricated world, and by projecting their imaginations into the world of fantasy. Development of the spiritual world will often occur more subtly through the attitudes and values generated. Adults have an obligation at all times to avoid sex and race stereotypes.

Children will generally have plenty of things to express but occasionally they need an idea. Adults will find their suggestions most acceptable to children when they build upon direct experience or observation. It is generally advisable to use an open-ended idea that will cause each child to think and choose a more specific, personal aspect. The following partial list of themes may be useful in stimulating children's pictorial expression:

- I am going to the store to buy . . .
- My friends and I like to . . .
- If I could do anything I wanted, I would . . .
- Today I helped my mother/father by . . .
- In my land of make-believe, I saw . . .
- When I went to the zoo, I watched . . .
- This is my house
- I went to visit . . .
- When we drove across the desert, I saw . . .
- Today I saw baby birds in the nest outside my window
- God loves me because . . .

It is important for adults to try to feel what the child is trying to express before making additional suggestions. If it becomes apparent that a child has a specific interest, parents can encourage additional ways to use the pictures produced. Some children like to combine pictures in a booklet illustrating a series of events, a favorite book or story, or to illustrate an original story. Likewise, a series of pictures can be attached in sequence to create a simple box movie. If several children are involved, each can illustrate various portions. If captions are needed for a booklet or movie, which children are unable to write, adults should not write directly on the child's drawing. In the case of a booklet, the child's statement can be placed effectively on a facing page. For the movie, a strip can either be added below the drawing or the pictures can be pasted to a long, continuous strip of paper which is wider allowing for writing below each picture.

Another group project is a mural. By definition, a mural is a panel created as wall decoration which often condenses more ideas or activities in the mural space than could possibly occur in real life. For children, their neighborhood, a farm, a zoo, or other familiar themes are suitable.

Design activities share top priority with picture making for countless children. In many cases, instead of trying to depict the real world, young children paint designs. If one observes young children painting at easels, one observes that these children may be completely engrossed in creating patterns without ever showing any evidence of attempting to depict real people or things. Their patterns are often beautifully composed to fit the space and reveal effective use of color.

As children develop they maintain a strong sense of design in their paintings and drawings. Gradually as awareness of things around them grows, they incorporate symbolic images in their design compositions. For example, flowers may assume a highly decorative character. An apple tree may become a highly repetitive pattern of apples spaced along branches instead of appearing in the normal state of growth. As their symbolic forms develop for familiar aspects of the environment, the decorative quality prevails, giving individuality to each child's work.

Adults can encourage the decorative quality of children's work in a number of ways, but we will suggest only a few to illustrate. One helpful idea to promote with children is that of *letting the design grow* to fill the entire space. This concept of growing can be developed by the following method which becomes a kind of game to be played. Instruct children, after choosing a single crayon and holding it at the left side of their paper (on the right side if left-handed), to close their eyes and move across the paper in one continuous wavy or loopy line. Then opening their eyes and using other colors, start from the most prominent hump or loop in the line, what shows strongest, and let the design literally grow. Nothing is to be placed on the paper except as it grows from the preceding portion. Adults will quickly recognize that closing the eyes merely sets the mood and creates the game atmosphere. In essence, this idea helps children grasp the relationships essential to good design and gets away from putting something in the center and four corners of the paper. If the paper were larger, such a design could continue to grow. (See Art Processes Guide.)

Another design concept that can be developed readily is that of *repetition*. One of the simplest ways to develop this is through the use of cut paper. When paper is folded once, two halves will be identical but reversed. When folded twice, one achieves a four part pattern. The only help most children need is to be aware of the folds, cutting in at intervals, but never cutting away the entire fold. The snowflake described in a previous chapter is an example of six-part design pattern. (See Art Processes Guide.)

The principle of *positive-negative* prevails in many aspects of art and generally fascinates children. In its simplest aspect, a form cut from a folded paper is the "positive" while the remaining paper is the "negative." Another way of discovering this is to start from one edge of a rectangle, cutting in a continuous irregular path, without removing any paper, until the opposite edge of the paper is reached. The two pieces, when mounted on rectangles of another color, reveal exact opposites in design. As children explore this concept more intricately they can discover how to expand a shape, such as a square

or circle, to achieve a more complex relationship. (See Art Processes Guide.)

Many aspects of nature can be used to produce attractive designs. Leaves, flowers, fruits, trees, birds, butterflies, animals, other forms can be treated decoratively. Many children will create designs very naturally while others may benefit from observing designs in fabrics, wallpapers, or in other places, and then being stimulated to develop their own versions. For young children, the idea of fairy flowers, dream landscapes, fantastic animals, people from Mars, or other suggestions may stir their imaginations. Once adults show their respect for children's design efforts, many more ideas will be forthcoming. For many children who find it more difficult to create "real"-looking drawings, design is a wonderful creative outlet.

If children continue to use the same materials over a period of time, they may benefit from a suggestion to try another approach. If they have used crayons and tempera paints regularly, they may enjoy chalk, oil crayons, cut paper, torn paper, or felt markers. Any medium should be used directly without the use of pencil outlines. Adults should never let their own inhibitions and fears about the direct use of materials influence the normal freedom of children. A few specific processes may be identified that relate to picture making and design experiences offering new approaches.

PUTTING IT ALL TOGETHER

## Collage

A form of art known as collage is related to picture and design production but offers interesting variations for children to enjoy. A collage is an abstract or symbolic portrayal of ideas or feelings created with a wide assortment of materials attached to a piece of heavy paper or light cardboard. It is essentially two-dimensional though some materials may project from the background surface. We should not think of a collage as just another picture cut out from different materials and pasted together, but rather as a symbolic representation of the essence or heart of an idea, a kind of suggestion. A collage has been called "a feeling and seeing picture." Any kind of material that can be fastened to the base can be used. Fancy papers, cellophane, ribbon, lace, rickrack, fabric scraps, braid, string, yarn, leather scraps, pieces of bark, paper clips, weeds, grasses, twigs, and many other items offer possibilities. Materials can be pasted, taped, stapled, wired, sewed, or fastened in any conceivable manner. Making a collage is an excellent follow-up of the texture exploration described in Chapter 4.

A few examples will serve to illustrate the possibilities. A child who liked to play baseball used a miniature bat, a mitt cut from an old leather purse and a ball made from paper and marked to indicate stitching to create his baseball collage to hang in his room. A child who helped plant a garden used empty seed packets, paper strips folded like furrows and cut out a paper watering can for her gardening collage. Many children enjoy using a variety of interesting materials from their accumulated scrap collections to create purely decorative, abstract compositions.

Tissue collage offers another variation. Pictures or designs are formed by *tearing* pieces of colored tissue paper and adhering them in overlapping fashion to a piece of heavy paper or light cardboard. Children need to be shown how to lay a piece of tissue in place, then with a large brush dipped in a mixture of one part white glue and two parts water, brush across the *surface* of the tissue. The glue solution penetrates the tissue holding it to the background paper. Layer after layer is adhered in this manner. When dry, additional details may be added with felt markers or brush and paint if desired. Make certain that all brushes are washed immediately before the glue mixture has a chance to dry in the bristles.

## Gadget Printing

Another mode of expression which offers challenge is gadget printing. The materials needed are thick tempera paints, paper and a variety of gadgets. Prepare a simple ink pad by saturating a pad of folded paper towelling, soft cloth, cotton or felt with tempera paint in a shallow saucer or plastic lid. A great variety of objects—thread spools, bottle caps, corks, kitchen utensils, sticks, pieces of sponge, beads, heads of large nails or screws, and countless other items—are pressed on the saturated pad and printed. Designs can be created by repetition of motifs, overlapping of diverse forms and by interesting variations of textures.

In similar fashion, patterns can be created by wrapping a small block of wood with string, pressing it on the paint pad, and printing it in a variety of patterns. As children discover the excitement of printing various objects to create patterns they will come up with other methods.

## Crayon Etching

This intriguing process offers children variation from picture and design activities but uses the familiar wax crayon. For this purpose, one needs to select rather small pieces of heavy paper, tagboard (old file folders are excellent) or lightweight, smooth surfaced cardboard. Children often enjoy using variations in size and shape such as long, narrow pieces (approximately 2 or 3 inches wide by 7 or 8 inches long), squares, or circles. A piece of newspaper should be placed on the working surface to catch crayon chips. The entire pieces are covered with random, repeated patches of many colors, which must be colored *very heavily* and *solidly* so no paper shows through. When the entire surface is filled, it is covered with a second layer of a single color, also colored solidly. Although black is often chosen, interesting effects may be achieved from using brown, purple, grey, or a metallic crayon such as silver or bronze if available in the child's crayons. The necessity for pressing and coloring heavily explains why the piece of tagboard should be rather small. Because the color patches may be of any size or shape, the process is helpful in promoting muscular development.

After the color preparation is completed, the object is to scratch away bits of the surface color to create a pictorial or design image. Children can experiment with various scratching tools—the head or point of a large pin or nail, bobby pin, nail file, paper clip, orange stick, or other object which does not pose danger to the child. Often children are quick to discover that they can color over parts as needed. It should be noted that the under colors revealed will be softer because the wax is scratched away leaving only the color stain on the paper surface. Many themes or ideas can be employed effectively, but fantasy is particularly appropriate for colors appear at random and seldom match real hues of objects.

## Crayon Resist

Another use for paint and crayons involves the principle that a waxy surface resists water. Children can create all kinds of line designs on paper making certain that large amounts of paper are left uncolored and that all crayon lines are heavily drawn. Next a thin mixture of tempera paint or transparent watercolor is washed across the surface with a large brush.

I recall a group of first graders who gave a name to this resist technique. Winter had been long and cold, but spring and Easter were approaching. In an effort to stimulate them, I had drawn large flowers on white paper with white crayon. Then as I painted across the paper with thin color, the flowers suddenly appeared. One child excitedly called it "magic painting" and the name stuck. This group explored the process with great enjoyment. But the real significance of the experience was revealed the following October when these same children were drawing Halloween pictures. One child asked me if she could have some black paint and a brush. Later she proudly revealed her eerie picture. She had drawn ghosts with white crayon and painted over them with the black paint to create the effect she desired. Whenever we observe that children choose a particular process at a later date to fit a particular need, we know they are learning to think visually.

Picture making and design can certainly be regarded as the most common forms of expression and can be used by children to express their ideas in relation to their worlds: the human world, the natural world, the fabricated world, the imaginary world and the spiritual world. However, there are innumerable other forms of expression that can be enjoyed by children and should be encouraged. Before suggesting some other approaches, we need to consider what criteria to use in determining appropriate choices for young children.

## Judging Alternative Choices

In considering other forms of artistic expression for children let us ask the following questions:

- Are the materials *safe* for children to use?
- Can children work *independently* with the chosen materials, after basic procedures are shown, without relying on adults to do it for them?
- Does the process encourage *originality* rather than rigid step-by-step making of trite forms?
- Will both the *working process* and *final product* be important means by which children can express their *own* ideas?

It would be impossible to suggest every means of expression appropriate for young children. Therefore, several suggestions have been selected to guide adults in helping children develop. In every situation, the child's own unique personality and interests must be considered first. Although children may reject suggestions at one point, they may accept them enthusiastically at another time. Building on children's immediate interests and experiences will always be more successful than trying to force something strange on them. In some cases, by offering children several suggestions from which to choose, adults demonstrate their interest and approval of children's efforts without dictating or demanding specific results.

## *Construction Activities* (See Art Processes Guide)

Many children thoroughly enjoy putting forms together from a variety of materials. Three-dimensional construction offers endless possibilities with simple materials to involve children productively. Boxes of every size, corrugated cartons (ranging from small ones to huge ones used in shipping mattresses, furniture and appliances), paper tubes, heavy cardboard tubes, large pieces of fabric, can stimulate the imaginations of children endlessly. Sometimes children combine cartons with existing pieces of furniture to create an imaginary *play-space*. They may reconstruct this area almost daily, changing it to respond to the play situation involved. Adults should observe such activity with interest, show willingness to listen if children want to share, but respect the privacy involved. Obviously, this process of creating is a lively, energetic one allowing little permanency of the product.

Another form of construction centers around the making of *buildings*. Some enjoy using various cartons and boxes to create houses and other buildings. If interest is sustained over a longer period or if several children are involved, a town or city, a farm, or possibly an imaginary location can be developed. I recall that a first grade group studying their neighborhood decided to construct a model from cartons. Each chose a particular building to make and used great ingenuity in adding details. Cartons of the size used for canned goods were used for most structures. Houses were made by cutting the end flaps in triangular shape for the gabled end before adding other cardboard for the roof. One little boy making a gas station made gas pumps very cleverly using toilet tissue tubes and braided string for the hoses. With encouragement, children think of countless ways of creating trees, shrubbery, and other details.

Some children prefer to construct the inside of a house or building furnishing it with miniature furniture and equipment. Because many young children have not achieved finer muscle coordination, adults should take their cue from the child's own inclination toward detail rather than forcing it before the child is ready. Part of the pleasure derived from such activities occurs in the daily changes children make during their play.

In like fashion, children can use similar materials to construct *vehicles*. Some will use existing vehicles, such as wagons, to create their own special vehicles. Others will make smaller objects. We should respect their efforts, however crude, if they show originality of purpose. This is not the time to purchase model kits which a child is not ready to construct.

*Box animals* can be developed readily by children. From a wide variety of shapes and sizes, they can have fun creating their own varieties. I recall a child who called his creation an "eledog" because the front end looked like an elephant and the rear end like a dog.

Scrap wood can provide many happy hours for children. In some instances, a flat piece of wood can serve as a base to which the child can attach other pieces of various shapes in creating a *wall plaque*. White glue is a suitable adherent. Young children can develop a very genuine sense of design when selecting and arranging such a wall panel. When the glued pieces are thoroughly dry, the effectiveness may be enhanced by spraying the entire surface with a single color, such as white, black, gold or a specific color. Some will be more attractive if left in the natural wood state. Observation of works of artists may help children decide how to finish their own creations.

Wood pieces can also be used to construct *free-standing forms*. Encouraging children to test out arrangements which are balanced so that they can stand without falling over challenges their ingenuity. Once the basic form is completed, a variety of additional details may be added from materials previously collected such as beads, string, yarn, buttons, small machinery parts, and the like. If children show inclinations toward three-dimensional constructions they can be encouraged to create other forms using an ever greater diversity of materials. The term, *stabile*, can be added to their vocabularies.

*Mobiles* offer still another exciting direction involving construction. Two aspects are important in making mobiles: balance and movement. Simple mobiles can be developed using a base form such as a tree branch of interesting shape, a coat hanger, or a shaped piece of heavy cardboard. From this form can be suspended a great variety of objects. Cut paper forms, small balls, tiny boxes, small machine parts, other forms must be placed so as to balance other objects and to move freely when the mobile is hung without striking other forms. If children begin with simple mobiles, their interest may continue in later years to more complex types.

## *Puppets* (See Art Processes Guide)

Because children love make-believe, they enjoy puppets. Some children have seen elaborate marionette shows but these figures operated by strings are far too difficult for them to make. To avoid frustration in young children, adults need to guide them in learning simple puppet-making processes through which they can express their individuality. Among the many methods possible, we need to find those which can actually be made by young children themselves, not by adults for them to use in play. It should be noted that puppets are operated from below while marionettes or string puppets are handled from above. The suggestions that follow may inspire still other useful approaches.

*Stick puppets* are the most rudimentary. The child draws a figure, mounts it on light cardboard, cuts it out, and fastens it to a stick. Variations involve cutting out one leg separately and attaching it to the body with a paper fastener so it can move. A second shorter stick attached to the moveable leg allows movement such as walking. An arm can be treated similarly if necessary to the action.

*Hand puppets* are constructed basically of a head fitting over the middle finger or the whole hand and a body formed by covering the rest of the hand with cloth. The head is the most important and may be created using Styrofoam balls, rubber balls with a hole for the finger, or of cloth formed over a paper tube. Children can easily make a cloth head by using an eight inch square of cloth. After a face is drawn with crayon in one corner, it is gathered together, stuffed with soft material and formed and tied around a stiff paper tube which will fit over the child's middle finger. Hair, caps, hats, other details can be added readily. To operate these puppets, a piece of cloth is put over the finger before the head is placed on it. Thus a simple body plus a head makes an active puppet.

Another very simple form is a *paper bag puppet*. A rather small, square-bottomed sack is chosen. A face is drawn or painted on one side. Shredded paper or soft stuffing fills the head thus created. In using, it is tied around the child's wrist to create the effect of a neck. The lower part of the sack can be painted to resemble clothing if desired.

I have seen charming *animal puppets* created by kindergarten children from paper bags. The story of the "Three Little Kittens" was simply but effectively done by making each cat from two paper bags, one for the head and one for the body. Two rolled paper tubes made the legs, one roll over the body sack created the two front legs, the other the two hind legs. Another rolled paper tube made the tail. Children manipulated them by two strings, one attached to the head and one to the body near the tail. Again the important thing is to encourage children to use their ingenuity, not to show them our methods. Given a starting idea of how puppets operate, children may come up with better ideas than adults can generate. It is important to permit children to create their own puppets, however crude they may appear, rather than expect more sophisticated products.

*Paper sack birds* can readily be made for use in puppet plays or for other purposes. A flat envelope sack works best. One corner of the sack is stuffed with a small wad of paper letting the corner become the bill. String tied below the bill thus formed creates the head by indicating the neck. The body is formed by adding more stuffing, folding in the excess part of the sack, and tying again at the base of the body. The remainder of the sack, squeezed together, makes the tail. I have seen children add paper wings and one child even found suitably shaped twigs to insert for legs and feet. Another child devised an ingenious paper nest. Give children a chance and they will amaze you with their clever ideas!

## Creating Banners

Banners offer another form of expression children enjoy. Banners can be used for diverse purposes because of their colorful, decorative quality. Children in a primary school (ages 5 to 8) created marvelously effective banners to decorate their school. Many of their banners expressed their feelings about nature and the four seasons while others were pure design. As an initial step, they made banners of colored construction paper pasted to wrapping paper to try out their ideas. Later burlap was used for the banner itself by fringing the edges and fastening the top to a dowel stick to facilitate hanging. Designs were cut from colored felt and attached with white glue to the burlap base. Burlap, felt, cloth, ribbon, braid, buttons, other items are all potential banner materials.

Because of the historical significance of banners used both in religious ceremonies and to designate medieval craft guilds, this idea can offer added interest to children learning about the stories from the Bible and the symbolism used in religious observances. Banners, as well as drawings and paintings, may be created by children to depict well-known Bible stories such as Adam and Eve, Noah's Ark, Jacob's Ladder, Joseph and his Coat of Many Colors, David and Goliath, Daniel in the Lions' Den. Most important of all are the many events connected with the birth and life of Jesus. In every instance, children need to become thoroughly familiar with the story before they attempt to illustrate it. At this point, adults can help children understand what banners are and can guide their choice of materials to create them. But the banner or picture produced should be the result of the child's own interpretation, not a copy of a picture in a book, not an imitation of an adult's ideas and not made from patterns.

In connection with the making of banneeds, adults can help children observe some of the *symbols* associated with the Christian faith. Although the list could be very lengthy, let us note only a few examples which can be found in many churches that can be used to enhance children's understanding. The idea of *God the Father* is often expressed symbolically by the hand of God. *God the*

*Son* is variously designated by the fish, the lamb of God, or the candle expressing the light of the world. Both the dove and the flame are used to depict *God the Holy Spirit*. Likewise, the cross is an ever-present symbol found in many forms.

Other well-known symbols depict the four Evangelists. The winged man depicts St. Matthew, the winged lion represents St. Mark, the winged calf denotes St. Luke, while the eagle symbolizes St. John. Familiar nature forms have special Christian significance both in churches and in religious sculpture and paintings from past centuries. Those that can be more readily understood by children are: the bee showing activity, diligence, work; the butterfly signifying the resurrection; the dove for purity and peace; the eagle denoting the resurrection; the grain and grapes representing the bread and wine; the lily for purity; and the palm showing victory.

Banners incorporating symbols as well as natural forms can be used by children to express their feelings about themes such as God Is Love, The Lord Is My Shepherd, The Earth Is the Lord's, and to depict other values and beliefs they derive from their faith as they learn to praise God in their own appropriate ways. It is far more important to recognize children's own very personal interpretation than to encourage them to be imitators.

## Weaving Experiences

Weaving is a form of art that can promote another aspect of creative effort for children. The process is an ancient one common to people throughout the world, and its pursuit continues to attract many. In its simplest aspects, weaving involves crossing one fiber with another in an interlocking pattern to create useful and durable fabrics. Excavations of ancient sites have revealed weavings of both simple and complex structure.

Children need guidance in understanding how to move the weaver over and under the warp material, alternating row by row to create the necessary interlocking strength. Paper can be used in first efforts until children understand the process. Then their weaving can continue to expand to include a greater diversity of materials allowing them to make actual articles.

To introduce weaving, adults can help children fold and cut paper in parallel slits. When the paper is opened, weaver strips can be inserted in over and under patterns with appropriate alternation of rows. Later, variations such as over and under two can be discovered. An interesting change involves cutting a sheet of paper (at least 9 x 12 inches or larger) into an irregular pattern of slits and using weavers of different width and shapes. When completed the loose ends of the weavers should be pasted to hold the weaving intact.

Simple box, cardboard or frame looms can be made and warped with string or strong yarn. Children can learn to employ other materials for the cross weaving or weft. Strips of fabric, leather, natural grasses, yarns of varying thicknesses

*fold*

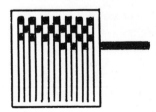

offer countless possibilities to the young weavers. Weaving offers excellent possibilities for use of the many materials which are discards from various industries as well as for those things collected and sorted out previously.

As children become more familiar with the principles of the weaving process, they may be encouraged to discover other applications of the technique. The crotch area of a sturdy forked branch offers a place for weaving. Such pieces of weaving can be incorporated in mobiles or other constructions effectively.

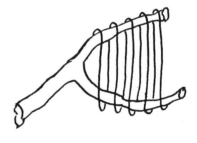

Examples of weaving can be identified and observed in numerous materials and objects of daily use such as rugs, draperies, clothing, baskets, but these applications are generally beyond the productive scope of young children. As children gain muscular coordination and show interest and readiness, methods for weaving simple circular mats and baskets may be sought.

## Modeling Activities

Children playing in sand at a beach will frequently be observed digging channels, building elaborate structures and devising systems that are intricately planned. Such three-dimensional shaping of pliable materials is both natural and beneficial to young children's muscular development and control, and stimulates their thinking and planning capacities. Many children similarly enjoy an outdoor or indoor sandbox and take great delight in making daily or very frequent changes.

*Non-hardening clay*, variously called modeling clay, plastiline or plasticene, which has an oil base, has been referred to previously under the discussion of materials. Many children enjoy creating expressive human or animal figures and will often incorporate them in various construction projects or models. Small plastic bags are useful for storing balls of clay both to keep them free from dust and to reduce drying out. If *water based clay* is being used, it can be kept moist in plastic bags during working but should be allowed to air dry completely before any painting occurs. Sudden exposure to heat is apt to cause cracking and breaking. Broken clay can be re-soaked in water, kneaded and blended for reuse only if no foreign matter such as paint or glue has been applied.

Sometimes children wish to model a form which will be more durable than fragile clay. Of the various possibilities available, papier mâché is deemed the most suitable. (See Art Processes Guide.) For activities of this nature, it is often desirable for adults and children to work together. For example, if the material tends to stick to a child's small hands, the adult can suggest using a damp sponge to reduce stickiness from fingers. Modeling forms, though highly satisfying when completed, can offer greater frustration during the working process.

*Papier mâché* should be recognized as a highly versatile material that often facilitates solving construction problems. Although papier mâché can be employed in either pulp or strip form, the latter is much more readily handled. Essentially, we are dealing with *torn* strips or pieces of absorbent paper (newspaper, toweling, tissue) which are dipped in a paste solution and applied to varied surfaces. Such a coating, when dry, is very light in weight and amazingly strong. In box construction, previously described, surfaces may be coated to change the texture, cover labels or printing on cartons, or to modify shape. For example, if children wish to change a flat surface to a curved or bumpy one, they can hold small pieces of *crumpled* paper in place, coat them with two to four layers of papier mâché and allow to dry. The final surface can then be painted as desired.

If paper bag puppets, animals or birds need greater detail or a more durable finish, they can be coated with papier mâché strips very effectively. The possibilities are limitless depending only on the child's personal skill to achieve. In many cases, the most rudimentary forms will fully express the child's own appropriate level of development and should be respected as such. But when children themselves feel the need for more complex portrayals, then adults can encourage more elaborate processes to satisfy their needs. (See Art Processes Guide.)

## Celebrating Holidays

The most natural and charming examples of how children celebrate will be found in the illustrations they draw or paint about various holidays and special days. As adults, we can become much more conscious of the *real* meaning these days have for children when we observe how they interpret them in their own inimitable ways. Often parents like to encourage children to make personal gifts for grandparents or other relatives and friends. What could be more genuine than a child's own painting or drawing? Instead of trying to find some article to be made as a gift, however dubious its actual use may be, we could encourage the child to choose a picture, perhaps mount it, and wrap it as a gift. The same consideration can be observed for other examples of genuine child art which may serve as more appropriate gifts from children than all the "clever" gadgets contrived in the name of gifts.

Original *greeting cards* can be created by children using many of the processes already described. Attractive designs appropriate to the holiday or special event can be made from drawing, painting, crayon resist, crayon etching, torn or cut paper, tissue collage, finger painting or other method. Parents may be able to guide children in selecting a suitable design or portion of a larger design to be mounted on a selected folded paper card and can assist them, if necessary, in writing the message inside. I have observed children ingeniously making cards with movable portions thus adding greatly to their personal message. Our wholehearted acceptance of children's creative effort in making cards is the true key to stimulation of further efforts.

Encouraging children to decorate their own rooms for various holidays as well as sharing in making other parts of the house festive is important to their artistic development. Although they should be allowed complete freedom in their own room decorations, they should be helped to understand that both adults and children occupy other parts of the house. Parents can plan with children how and where their contributions will be most effective. Banners may be attractive additions. Table decorations including centerpiece, placecards, simple favors offer great possibilities for children's efforts particularly for family events or children's own parties.

Whatever we do to observe holidays and special days, we should make certain that we have allowed children to express their ideas freely and that we have accorded them full respect for their contributions. We can stimulate and guide them toward new explorations and discoveries as they become more mature, but we must never attempt to steer their efforts toward trite or stereotyped products. Accepting what they produce with sincerity and love is vital to their best development and self-respect.

# 6

# Sharing for Growth
# and Mutual Understanding

WHEREVER ONE GOES THROUGHOUT THE WORLD one finds children producing art in surprisingly similar fashion. One observation repeatedly stands out relative to children's expression: children express most readily what they know best. Children from rural areas paint farm life as they know it, while the urban child readily shows buildings, vehicles in traffic, people, and activities associated with the city. Children who live near mountains depict them with understanding while those from desert areas express that arid landscape with surety. To suggest that children draw or paint what they have never experienced forces them to depend upon imitative processes. Sometimes adults become too eager for "new" and "different" ideas forgetting that what may seem commonplace to adults is new and exciting to children. If adults recognize that the ideas or subjects which children choose must be meaningful to them, then these adults will become more comfortable observing *how* they depict their choices and in discussing the art expression itself.

The earliest admonition for all adults is to remove entirely from their vocabularies the question, *"What is that?"* Immeasurable harm is done to children's eagerness to express themselves by this or other similar questions. If every adult would listen first to the child, then comment carefully later, many frustrations could be avoided. Children are eager to share their efforts and need approving reactions in order to grow in their artistic expression. This does not imply that adults should comment that everything is "beautiful" or "lovely," for children are quick to sense insincerity. But it does mean the cultivation of guarded comments until one learns first what the child intended. It takes patience and practice to learn to discuss creative efforts with children, but it brings rewards in the long run.

It has been noted previously that a child's first efforts involve *scribbling* or *manipulation* of materials. Adults should never obstruct a child's scribbling by suggesting something specific to be drawn. Scribbling involves motor control of materials rather than ideas. If, for example, parents suggest to their little girl that she draw an apple, her reaction is apt to be one of asking her parent to show her how. To a young child, an apple is to eat, not to draw! Why should she want to draw an apple since she can't eat a drawing? When children are ready to relate their scribbling to something of reality, they will name it themselves.

Frequently, the first named scribbles children make will relate either to themselves or to some special person. If the child says, "This is me," accept it even though it still looks like a scribble to you. If your child paints a crude person with a green face and purple hair, and says, "This is you, Mommy," accept it gracefully! The fact that your child chooses to paint you is a compliment worth more than the actual painting. By your recognition of the effort, you will stimulate further expression.

It is extremely important for children to sense acceptance. If your little boy says simply, "This is me," you can do much to extend *his* thinking by asking questions such as, "What are you doing?" "Where are you going?" or "Is someone helping you?" Avoid suggesting something specific or totally different, such as, "Why don't you draw our house?" for this may imply disapproval. Always take your cue from what the children tell you, then encourage the direction of *their* thinking with further open-ended questions that enable them to choose. Many adults have unhappy memories of school art lessons that were specifically directed toward prescribed results. These people are apt to belittle their own ability as a result. Such unfortunate experiences should not be repeated. With sincere adult encouragement, each child's unique qualities can emerge without the frustrations many adults have experienced.

The more adults become acquainted with children's early forms of art expression, the more readily they recognize children's efforts. However, there is always the danger of a wrong guess. Suppose little Tommy shows you his drawing and you mistakenly comment about his nice dog but he says it is a horse. Be quick to admit *your* error, accepting the fault graciously but not apologetically. Comments such as, "I can see his head is too long for a dog," or, "Of course, his legs don't look like a dog's," will encourage the child without damaging your credibility. Admitting a mistake can be far more damaging to a developing child than to a mature adult. Children feel sincerity readily, so adults must be particularly careful in controlling their comments. It is far better to listen first to what the child says, then add your words of encouragement, rather than be forced to retract an unfortunate remark.

If the groundwork is laid early for mutual understanding, it will become easier for adults to relate to the creative efforts of children with sensitivity and enjoyment. The more adults become familiar with the delightfully personal qualities of children's art, the greater will be their appreciation. Although the subject or idea depicted by children in different parts of the world will reflect their native environments, the *manner* in which they develop their expression will often be strikingly similar. As children move from scribbling through the naming of scribbling stage, they begin to develop symbols that may become highly sophisticated as they progress. Let us examine some of these conventions that are found repeatedly wherever children draw or paint and discover how to react to them.

# Characteristics of Children's Art Expression

## Children's Early Use of Color Is Not Necessarily Related to Objects

In observing a very young child's earliest efforts, one will generally note that a single color—any color—will be used. Children grasp crayons in their fists and scribble with full arm movement, gradually developing control. Sometimes another color will be added in another scribble, especially if the page is large, but the choice of color is basically accidental. Even when children begin to name the scribbles, color has little significance.

As children begin drawing or painting specific forms—people, pets, houses, trees, vehicles, others—the colors are not necessarily "real" in the sense of being directly related to the particular objects. Frequently children will use whatever color is available without concern. Adults must accept children's choices without comment. As children continue to develop, they may ask questions or show concern about specific hues. At this stage adults may guide their observations and experiments with color as suggested earlier under the discovery of art elements. Children should make their *own* reasoned choices and adults should not attempt to provide specific answers for them.

## Children Possess Innate Color Sense

All one needs to do is look at children's paintings to discover striking color combinations. Undoubtedly, nature is the only close rival to children in the exciting array of colors that is possible. In recent years, many designers have combined colors previously considered incompatible, such as, red and pink, blue and green, magenta and orange, and others. Children have used such color combinations with boldness and charm for ages without needing any "rules" to govern them. Although adults may be overwhelmed at first by the seemingly brash colors children employ, they need to withhold comment and observe and listen. Much of the charm of children's work can be traced to their remarkable and unhesitating command of pure color!

As one grows accustomed to the color combinations children use, one becomes more comfortable in talking about them. Often, by saying to a child, "I like your bright colors. Will you tell me about your painting?" you will release a whole outburst of exciting information. The role of the adult should be to lead the child to share information, not to close it off.

### Children Generally Show People in Front View

As adults observe the drawings and paintings of young children, they will discover that people will generally be drawn full face or front view. Side view, or profile, is far less common particularly among the earliest forms of expression. Symbols for people consist first of head, arms and legs. The body appears later. It is also interesting to note that children emphasize whatever part of the body is being used specifically. Arms performing a task may be larger and may have hands with fingers. The head is more apt to contain eyes and mouth than nose and ears. Similarly one can observe how children depict other parts of the body. Many times, after young children paint a large head, body and arms, they will compress the legs into whatever space remains on the paper rather than omit a part of the person.

Details painted or drawn by children reveal many interesting facts. If a girl has a new dress and a boy has a new shirt, they may draw or paint themselves with surprising detail. I recall an incident related to me by the mother of a first grader. The children had been making pictures of themselves and Mary tearfully insisted she *had* to wear the same dress the next day, even though soiled, so she could complete her picture. On another occasion, a second grader showed her teacher with gray hair and a pencil over her ear, exactly as she saw her daily.

Children draw and paint people freely until they develop frustrations from critical remarks or insensitive questions. When they reach the stage of needing help and information, they should be guided by adults but not shown how. Some adults who draw skillfully are tempted to show the child how to draw the item in question, or what is worse, actually draw it for them. A boy once asked me how to draw a boy batting a ball. I first asked him to show me how he would stand to bat a ball. Then I asked a classmate to take the position for him to observe. Such a process may not produce an immediate result, but it is a step in the direction of understanding and confidence rather than imitation and dependence.

## Children Use Sky Strip and Ground Strip Persistently

As children begin to combine elements in their pictures, they use representations common to children everywhere in the world. At the top will be a narrow strip of blue sky while across the bottom will be a strip of green grass. These elements will persist for a fairly long time in spite of facts the children may know. For example, in addition to the blue sky, there will usually be a sun, possibly clouds and even rain, all in the same picture. Children similarly use a green strip at the lower edge, sometimes with snow or a mud puddle resting on top of it. Individual children often develop highly personal symbols with their sky and grass strips. One little girl made every sun in her picture for weeks with a face and braids. Suddenly she volunteered to me that she didn't know why she made her sun that way and stopped abruptly.

The grass strip may be modified, but always there is some "base line" to form the ground or land. Children logically feel the sky above and the ground below them. I overheard an adult question a first grader about what was between sky and the ground. The little girl sweetly and confidently replied, "Air!"

In addition, most objects will be placed side-by-side on the base line. Houses, trees, flowers, people, other objects will frequently be placed on the base line but rarely overlapped. Only things flying above the ground will be seen in the air space —birds, butterflies, airplanes. I have often heard children say that their pictures are full when the ground space is filled even though considerable air space remains. Ideas of overlapping, sky meeting ground at the horizon will occur when children sense these phenomena for themselves, not because adults "tell" them to do it.

### Children Portray Depth and Distance in Unique Ways

Adults accept the fact that things *appear* smaller as they recede in space and that distance is represented by placing smaller objects higher on the page. Children have their own concept of space and distance and cannot comprehend formal perspective until they are mature. Characteristically children's work will reveal highly simplified ways of showing forms in space. Much of the charm of their work derives from their naive approach. A lake, a pond with ducks swimming in it, a skating rink with skaters will appear as a circular shape standing on end. A fenced area will appear as a circle with the posts following the shape of the circle. Children playing a circle game will likewise follow the circle around: those on the sides drawn with feet toward the circle and heads on the outside, those on the near side of the circle upside down. No child will be seen from the side or the rear, and none will overlap the others.

Sometimes, in an effort to show space, a child uses two base lines, one at the bottom, the other halfway up the picture space. Placing two aspects one above the other, each in full view is common. At times, in order to show both sides of a street, children will employ a kind of double or mirror-like plan, which, if folded, would allow each half of the street to stand upright.

Another device commonly used is that of showing outside and inside simultaneously. The outside of a house will be revealed in the shape of the structure, surrounding landscape, but as though the front were removed showing the interior rooms, their furnishings and activities. In somewhat similar fashion, time sequence may be shown by two or more events occurring within the single area of the picture space. At other times, the comic strip style of separate pictures is used.

In all of these examples, if adults will only take the time to *listen* to the child's version first, they will be amazed at the facility displayed by the child in depicting very simply and logically a very complicated idea. It is important to realize that these children are thinking and solving their problems on their own level and are not ready for adult concepts of space.

Early in my own teaching I followed the prescribed curriculum and taught a group of fourth graders a lesson in two-point perspective complete with vanishing points in which they drew a building. I thought that I had done a successful lesson until I discovered a week later that these children went right back to their own way of drawing buildings. They had fun with the lesson on the day it was done but it proved to be a false hope of equating pleasure with learning. They were unable to apply the principles to future work and could perform only when following step-by-step directions. Subsequent work with children proved to me repeatedly that understanding cannot be forced. I also learned that these formalized drawings were sterile in comparison to the delightful compositions made by children in their own way.

### Children Reveal a Strong Sense of Design

Adults are often attracted to the designs found in textiles, pottery, and other articles produced by people in primitive cultures. Children, if allowed to function naturally, often show a remarkable sense of pattern and design akin to those of primitive societies. Many times when observing children painting at easels, one will note that they are completely involved in developing color patterns in space abstractly. It is an error to expect all creative expression to depict objects one can identify. Arrangements of color and pattern have great appeal to children. Often when overly curious adults ask children *what* they are painting, I have heard the reply, "Just a design." Can it be that children are smarter than many adults in discovering how to ward off an unnecessary question?

During World War II a group of second graders, many of whose fathers were in the Pacific, had brought things to school sent to them from that area. Because the teacher's husband was also in the Pacific, they discussed the items and had a large map on the bulletin board identifying locations from which their gifts had been sent. A few days later, one boy was making what appeared to me to be a design in green, blue and pink. When I commented on his unusual design, he quickly informed me that it was a map. The three map colors and the strange shapes of islands were what he was able to grasp and he was interpreting them as a design.

When children draw pictures depicting experiences or events, they often complete them or "fill the space" by incorporating design elements effectively. Although some aspects may appear incongruous to the more literal-minded adult, the result should be respected for the ingenuity displayed. Design quality may be revealed in numerous ways. Some create pattern with rows of flowers, birds flying in the sky, apples on the branches of a tree, or waves on the lake, while others will accomplish it by lines, dots, or other abstract shapes.

We must always be cautious about making comments or judgments. In the early days of television, I made an interesting discovery about a second grade boy. As I was walking home one afternoon, Bobby's mother stopped me with the question, "What have you been teaching Bobby about lines in art?" I could recall nothing, but her question puzzled me. The next day Bobby handed me several small pieces of paper covered with very intricate line patterns made in pencil. I was more puzzled than ever, but rather than question him then or indicate any doubt that he had made them, I gave him a large sheet of paper and suggested he make a larger one in color. Within a short time, he produced a beautifully intricate pattern of wavy lines in various colors, spaced at varying intervals but never intersecting. After commenting enthusiastically I asked him where he got his idea. When he merely shrugged, I asked him where and when he made the first ones. His reply indicated that he made them at home while watching television. I never completely solved the puzzle except to recall that the black and white television reception often shifted into wavy line patterns on the screen. I could only guess that he captured this effect. The important thing was that I accepted his effort without ridicule and he was so pleased that he gave me his lovely design.

Children often depict familiar aspects of nature in beautifully decorative ways. I have seen apple trees made by children in patterns handsome enough to grace drapery fabrics. When one least expects it, a child may interpret an idea in design rather than realistically. A group of second graders had been discussing things done to prepare for winter. Many ideas such as raking leaves, harvesting crops, putting on storm windows, had been suggested. Suddenly Jimmy said, "I know. Squirrels gather nuts."

Jimmy chose an 18 x 24 inch sheet of paper and soon became very involved in his drawing. When he finished, he had very ingeniously made two huge trees loaded with squirrels. But unlike usual drawings, he made the tree trunks *green* so that the many brown squirrel holes and the bushy-tailed brown squirrels would show. The effect was strikingly decorative in depicting his idea clearly.

### Children Base Size Relationships on Importance

When children draw or paint several objects in one composition, they do not reveal true proportions in the adult sense.

For the child, what is most important at the moment will assume dominance over all the rest. It is not unusual to see flowers half as high as a house, windows and doors smaller than the people, and other similar discrepancies. A child may not depict what he knows, but rather what he feels. Gradually size relationships may take on greater importance. However, it should be noted that the use of distortion in art has been employed throughout the ages and can be an effective device for the young artist responding to his feelings as much as to the mature artist who chooses it deliberately.

When adults insist on "correct" proportions, they often cause severe frustration in children. Shirley, as a second grader, drew charming people and faces readily. One day she came to me in tears saying, "My daddy says I draw my faces all wrong." With careful questioning, I learned that her father, who was a highly accomplished artist/designer/inventor, tried to explain the proportions of the human face in terms of fractional divisions. Although Shirley was an intelligent child, she had no understanding whatever of fractions, but felt only that her father was critical of her work. The damage that was done to Shirley's confidence was irreparable and only by diverting her interest to totally new directions could I partially overcome her disillusion about her own art work.

The preceding characteristic qualities identified and described in children's drawings and paintings are all readily observable. Adults are urged to be aware of similar modes of expression in other creative work of children. Because three-dimensional works—puppets, mobiles, constructions, and the like—are more difficult to view and compare, the characteristics are not as quickly discernible. However, adults should be conscious of the same qualities in all expressive art and make their own observations using the same discretion in commenting about them.

In all of the foregoing examples, adults are reminded that children express their ideas in unique ways which should be respected and valued rather than discouraged. Children must experience for themselves, think for themselves, and express themselves in their own ways. If adults try to prescribe the expressive and creative acts of children, they will curtail their capacity to act independently and responsibly.

Many things children produce will fall into the category of experiments, valuable as learning tools, but scarcely worth preserving. On the other hand, some items will possess charm and quality worthy of display and retention. How can adults provide for such needs of growing children?

## Displaying Children's Work

It has already been pointed out that children need acceptance of their work by adults. Does this mean that parents should display everything a child produces? Hardly. The key response should be "selection" of appropriate examples. How then can this be accomplished?

Attention has been given previously to the provision of working space. It is highly desirable that this area include a small bulletin board or tacking area where a child can select and display work. Obviously there won't be room for everything at once so choices must be made. By observing what a child chooses, the adult can often gain valuable insight into the child's expressive interests and purpose. Comments are important so the child feels adult support.

Sometimes space for displaying a child's art may be available in a family room or recreation area. Because of the more intimate quality of such an area, the works of children can be effectively shown and enjoyed. Frequent changes will be possible and advisable for the interests of children change quickly with accompanying rapid skill development. Where there are both older and younger children, great care must be taken to accept the work of *each* child without making comparisons. Each must be recognized as an individual worthy of attention.

In many homes there are unused spaces which could become handsome children's galleries. Stairways can make intimate

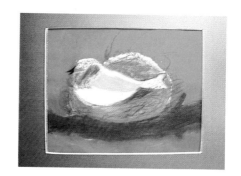

NESTING BIRD—*pastel*
Susan Sims
Grade 2
Jamesville, NY

WINTER BIRD
*Construction paper, crayon*
Tony Howell, Grade 2
Convoy, OH

THE GIRAFFE
AT THE ZOO
*Marker*
Carin Simmons
Grade 1
Convoy, OH

Courtesy Lutheran Brotherhood ANNUAL NATIONAL JUNIOR LUTHER-AN ART AWARD COMPETITIONS, Joan Sheldon McCargar, Fine Arts Coordinator

SNOW MONSTER
*Crayon and paint*
Philip Roth, Grade 2
Ottawa, IL

A WINTER SCENE
*Pencil and markers*
Colin Poellot
Tully, NY

SKATELAND—*crayon*
Kimberly Johnson
Grade 2
Canoga Park, CA

OCTOPUS—*yarn*
Andrew Seltz
Grade 3
Dearborn, MI

BOO—*felt-tip markers*
Christa Eichberger
Grade 2
Dearborn, MI

SPOOKY FACES
*Felt-tip markers*
Karl Schultz
Grade 2
Dearborn, MI

BUTTERFLY BRIGHT
*Wax scratch*
Lara Ann High
Grade 1
Cazenovia, NY

THE FARM AT NIGHT
*Markers*
Gretchen Smith
Grade 3
Eau Claire, WI

THE NEIGHBORHOOD
*Tempera and markers*
Bror Stark
Dearborn, MI

UNTITLED
*Found object*
Kathy Kent
Grade 3
Dearborn Heights, MI

ALL DRESSED UP
*Pastel*
Jenny Maynard
Grade 1
Dearborn Heights, MI

DANIEL IN THE
LIONS' DEN
*Watercolor*
Janet Ann Rider
Grade 2
Kaneohe, HI

MY FAVORITE PLAYGROUND
*Marker*
Kristin Berger
Grade 2
Canton, MI

SPACE 9
*Felt marker*
Nathan Aune
Kindergarten
Northfield, MN

OUR SCHOOL
BUILDING
*Crayon*
Kelly Martorelli
Grade 1
Fort Lauderdale, FL

ANGELS AND SHEPHERDS
*Tempera*
David Iverson
Grade 1
Fayetteville, NY

I LOVE JESUS
*Crayon*
Sheila Jane Gohil
Kindergarten
Fulton, MO

NOAH'S ARK
*Watercolor*
Scott Starks
Grade 1
Kailua, HI

HOUSE—*crayon*
Susan Dykes
Grade 3
Fort Lauderdale, FL

ANIMAL—*clay*
Michael Matias
Grade 2
Inkster, MI

UNTITLED—*weaving*
Amy Gustafson
Grade 3
Poplar, WI

viewing possible. In such places, parents may discover that simple framing enhances the work and provides protection from damage caused by movement in close quarters. A simple buttonback frame allows work to be changed frequently. A mat cut to fit standard paper size facilitates changes and adds to the appearance of the art work. Although parents may feel certain works are choice treasures to be saved, they may find it best to preserve them in other places and keep examples changing frequently in the family living areas to reflect the growth of their children's artistic endeavors.

A child's own room is a highly desirable location for the child's art to be displayed. In addition to those that may be hung on a wall, bulletin board, fastened to a door, or other flat surface, space should be available for three-dimensional work. Shelf space, a small table, or other surface at the level of the child's vision can be used effectively. Children should be encouraged at all times to accept responsibility for the appearance of their rooms and the effective display of their art can contribute greatly.

Although the kitchen is a much used area of every home, it should not be the only place where children's art is seen. Magnetizing a child's drawing to the refrigerator door may not be the best recognition of your child's effort. However, a special location in the breakfast area may receive daily recognition as the art examples add charm to the family meal. Parents should not be expected to remove examples of artists' work from their living room or dining room walls and replace them with children's art. Children need to see and appreciate the work of recognized artists as they build their own personal expression. Both have an important place in family life.

As their work develops, children may begin to experience self-consciousness about their work and disapproval of their earlier efforts. Parents are encouraged to preserve examples of work for future review. How can this be accomplished most advantageously?

## Continuous Evaluation of Children's Art

Because of the fragile quality of much of the paper that children use, such as newsprint, it is recommended that work to be saved be kept as flat as possible. Work will be more easily damaged if folded or rolled. An artists' supply store can provide large flat portfolios but the cost can be lessened greatly by the construction of home-made portfolios. Large sheets of corrugated cardboard used in boxes and in packaging appliances, furniture, mattresses and the like can be employed effectively. Sometimes a large, flat box can be located which will serve admirably. Scoring a large piece of corrugated cardboard to create a flat folder is the simplest form. Covering it with cloth or other material makes a more attractive folder.

It is suggested that the parent or the child label work on the *reverse* side showing date and appropriate comments. Adults are admonished strongly to avoid placing any writing on the *face* of a child's work. The child should learn how an artist signs a work making the signature an integral part of a composition. Words appear in art only as essential elements of a composition planned by an artist. Words, comments, letter grades, however approving in adult intent, actually serve to deface the child's effort, and should never be put on the front of any work.

Periodically, it can be beneficial to both children and adults to look back over art work previously done. I remember a particularly effective first grade teacher who always requested a folder of art work from me for each child to use during parent conferences. She related many instances where parents held a rather dim view of their child's art ability until shown actual work. In one case a child's drawing of the family kitchen truly amazed her mother when she observed how clearly her daughter observed minute details such as the mixing faucet, the light fixture and the refrigerator door opening.

When there are children of different ages in the family, much can be accomplished by way of mutual appreciation. I recall a fifth grade boy who ridiculed his little sister's efforts until his mother pulled out a folder of his work when he was her age. He then became her staunchest defender. Children who begin to lose confidence in their own efforts can develop new enthusiasm when they review work and discover their progress. Evaluation of efforts can also be effective in helping children discover that they need to learn new information or new ways of working. A child who loves to draw a specific thing, such as horses, may be inspired to study more about horses in order to become more skillful. I recall a young girl who was so crazy about horses that she read every book she could find, looked at pictures and the real thing whenever possible. She soon became very adept at drawing horses. Such an urge must come from within the child. It cannot be forced from outside. The ability to express oneself is contingent upon knowing fully what one wishes to express. If children are sufficiently inspired to create, they will develop the skills to accomplish what is necessary for fulfillment.

All children can benefit greatly from learning to express themselves visually. Only a small number will join the ranks of practicing artists but many will continue their enjoyment for a lifetime. Visual competency is a necessary element in total development of all human beings. Parents deprived of this aspect of their own education should guarantee it for their children by their open and thoughtful respect for their children's efforts.

# 7

# Relating to
# the World of Art

ON MANY OCCASIONS when I have visited art museums throughout the United States and in other countries as well, I have observed entire families viewing art together. I have seen babies in strollers, in backpacks, carried by parents, or toddling along, plus older children accompanying adults. How exciting it is to realize that seeing art is a natural part of these children's daily lives. Although only a relatively small proportion of these children will pursue art as their vocation, all of them will become adult consumers of art in every aspect of their lives. And what better way to begin than by getting acquainted with the world's great art, both from past ages and the present, in our art museums?

Undoubtedly, the key to lasting enjoyment and understanding is constant exposure. For parents who regularly visit art museums, it is natural to share the experience with their children from a very early age. But for adults who have not discovered the enjoyment and stimulation derived from viewing art, there may be considerable trepidation about knowing how to engage in the experience. We suggest that this can become an exciting adventure for the entire family, where all can learn together. Let us look at ways in which adults can learn to enjoy and appreciate art as they share their experiences with their children.

Attendance at art museums shows a remarkably high figure when ranked among the many forms of recreational activities available. In many cases admission is free, free on certain days, or offered for nominal fee or voluntary contribution, making museum-going far less costly for families than many other public events. Generally speaking, art museums are readily accessible and offer facilities designed to care for viewers' comforts during their visits. With these considerations in mind, we can urge parents to make frequent visits to art museums a regular part of family life.

If the first recommendation of regular visits is heeded, then the second follows naturally. Choose only a limited portion of an art museum to view during each visit. If you try to look at everything, you *see* very little. An important part of intelligent viewing is to cultivate the ability to see because art is primarily a visual experience. If your immediate reaction is to wonder just what you are *supposed* to see, consider how your senses operate in other facets of your life. Your senses enable you to react to your environment. You *hear* all manner of sounds which may be translated into mere noise or affect you as speech, drama or music. You *smell* fragrant flowers, the aroma of food, or become aware of the odor of dangerous substances. You *taste* various foods, relishing some, rejecting others. You *touch* diverse surfaces, responding appropriately. But do you question what you should hear or smell or taste or feel? Someone may guide you to try a new aspect but essentially you must reach your own complete response as you combine sensory impressions, feelings and thought. Your eyes react constantly to visual stimuli and your appreciation of the art you view must occur within you as you learn to see, feel and think.

Let us assume that you have entered a room in an art museum where paintings are displayed. What painting do you find yourself drawn to for viewing more carefully? What do you notice first? Is it an object or shape, a powerful color, an empty space, dynamic line, or some other feature? Try to observe how your eye travels as you study it more carefully. How often does your eye return to the point of initial impact? Consider how the artist employs the basic elements and principles of art (discussed in Chapter 4) to involve you, the viewer. Look at the work from a distance as well as at close range to observe its effectiveness. After such careful scrutiny you may discover that you do not have to "like" the painting to become involved in feeling its impact.

Crucial to appreciation of art is the recognition that the expressive impact or content of a work of art is *not* dependent on the subject matter. The mere choice of a subject is no guarantee that the work will be art. Likewise, the selection of a specific medium does not automatically create art. Only if the artist succeeds in controlling the elements and principles of art in a manner that is unique and personal can the results possibly become art. At this point it may be helpful to observe how various artists treat the same subject (e.g. a person, a house, a tree) with entirely different visual effects. With more visual involvement, you may begin to recognize that you may be more deeply affected emotionally and thoughtfully by paintings whose subject matter repels you than by those whose themes are pleasant.

The latter discovery can be an important means of understanding what works appeal to children. When children look at art, they are more apt to be attracted by bold color, strong composition, and movement than by pretty or pleasant subjects. Unlike many adults, they do not view art in terms of what to hang on the living room wall, but rather they react directly to the visual impact. Too often, adults have attempted to select for children what they, as adults, consider pleasant. If we watch children's reactions thoughtfully, we may discover preferences that shatter our previous notions. After we have let them have ample free exposure to various forms of art, we should take our cue from their demonstrated choices, recognizing that their views are not necessarily the same as ours.

As children are looking at art, we can ask them which painting or other art form they noticed most as they entered the room. Then we can find out what they observed about it—colors, shapes, lines, feeling, other qualities. One should be careful to talk about a work only as long as the child's interest prevails but not continuing to a point of fatigue. After a visit, parents can discuss with children what each one remembered most and why. On later visits, as children become more familiar with an art museum, they can choose what they wish to see first. Then a sensitive parent might guide them to another area which could serve to reinforce the child's selections or offer a contrasting approach.

A special caution is pertinent to viewing art. In their search for understanding of works of art, many adults take comfort in a "story" which may be related about the work. Artists are often reluctant to discuss their works though many acknowledge nature or the environment as being their chief source of inspiration. It is rare for artists to relate stories about their own work and it has been discovered frequently that such popular stories have been fabricated as convenient illustrations by someone other than the artist and often long after the death of the artist. Only when an artist specifically selects an event or person in history to depict or becomes the illustrator of a literary work does the story aspect have credence. Children and adults may create their own personal stories about a work of art based on the visual impact which stimulates their thinking, but that is quite a different reason.

Although adults often enjoy learning about the life of an artist, they should not rely on such information for appreciation. Unfortunately, more people know that Vincent van Gogh cut off his ear than fully appreciate his paintings. For very young children, even the name of the artist will have little value. Their concern is primarily visual. When children exhibit natural curiosity about the artist, they can be provided with pertinent information which may help them appreciate the artist as a real person but they should be spared unnecessary and possibly sordid details.

Many adults are extremely vocal in their dislike for so-called "modern" art and add the claim of "knowing what they like." The art of any period of history reflects the society of the time as well as pointing to innovation and change. At any given time, whether in the 16th or in the 20th century, the art produced could have been termed "modern." Artists living and producing art today cannot be expected to imitate the art of the past. They must react to their own society, utilize the materials and technology available, and produce what they feel honestly and sincerely expresses themselves. Children often react more readily to contemporary art forms than to the art of the past because it reflects the only world they know.

Neither adults nor children should be forced to "like" all forms of art, but both can develop open-mindedness in gaining understanding. Works of art can be compared to people. Sometimes, the person who seems most attractive in first meeting has little more to offer in closer association. But the person who was not as appealing initially may be discovered to have the lasting qualities that become richer as appreciation grows. As we come to "like what we know," we can discover for ourselves that our preferences for art forms change with understanding and we can then guide our children toward more reasoned choices. We should never be afraid to change our minds after contemplating works of art over a period of time.

In addition to viewing art in museums, we should note some of the special programs designed for children. In many areas, art museums, natural history museums, science museums are providing a variety of direct experiences for children designed to stimulate their senses. Some provide special rooms where children are allowed to experience many sensual stimuli from feeling objects, experimenting with light and sound, constructing spaces, seeing simulations of outer space, playing on special apparatus, all in a play atmosphere. Others offer special classes where children learn to create art freely in an atmosphere of varied art forms. Movement, dance and drama activities are emphasized in others as a means of stimulating children's responses. Programs of this kind offer two valuable opportunities for children. They can be sought in terms of class participation which children attend on a regular basis, a plan best suited to slightly older children who have demonstrated a definite interest. On a more sporadic basis, experience rooms provide an exciting interlude for young children whose parents can enjoy a more sustained period of gallery viewing than children are able to undertake.

An exciting experience area is provided in the Explore Gallery of the National Collection of Fine Arts (part of the Smithsonian Institution) in Washington, D.C. They also provide improvisational tours for children in which they view works of art as inspiration for feeling-into-movement activities. I observed another interesting program in the Midlands Art Centre of Birmingham, England where parents and children explored together such media as paint, clay, wood.

Art reproductions and books provide other sources for learning about art. When we visit museums we generally find a shop selling, among other items, reproductions of works of art from postcard size to large scale replicas. Although they provide valuable aids in recalling work for study, they can never compete in quality with the original works for full appreciation. Improvements in photographic techniques have brought improved reproductive quality, but the full richness of color and texture are difficult to attain. If children enjoy particular works they may enjoy owning a reproduction of their own. Books on art usually employ both color and black and white reproductions but the same limitations are always present. Once parents and children enjoy contacts with original works of art, they will recognize that there can be no adequate substitute for the real thing. Such awareness will certainly engender repeated contact with original works in art museums.

Book illustrations offer another aspect of art that can fascinate children. The quality of illustrations in books for children has improved through the expanded technology of mechanical reproduction. Naturally, children will gain ideas from the styles they observe, but they should never be encouraged or allowed to copy book illustrations. It is very important that, as adults, we recognize and stress with children the fact that it is wrong to copy a creative artist in any area of art. We do not copy a piece of music, a story, a poem, or a work of art and sign our name to it claiming it as our own. The presence of commercial kits on the market from which duplicate paintings may be made doesn't make the process right. Plagiarism is as wrong in the visual arts as in literary works.

Children need to be helped to appreciate artists as important people in our society who make worthwhile contributions. If we stress only art of past ages, children are apt to feel that artists are not living, breathing people like themselves. If adults watch for opportunities, they can often find places to take children where artists are at work. Some communities have art fairs where artists and craftsmen demonstrate for the public. Although some artists are not at ease with observers, especially young children, many of them welcome the chance to create increased public awareness. Sometimes parents will find it possible to have children meet a local artist personally. And children are truly fortunate if an artist takes a specific interest in children's groups, encourages their visits, or provides instruction as they grow older. Initial contacts made when children are young can help to increase their respect in the future for artists as productive members of their community.

What would our world be like without art and artists? When we consider that every aspect of our living can be connected to some degree with art in its myriad forms, we can conclude that there couldn't be such a world, or if it did exist, we would not want to inhabit it. We have emphasized that the first efforts of very young children, from scribbling to more complex expression, are worthy of our acceptance. Every young child who is respected for sincere, personal effort is learning to develop a balanced personality which can continue into mature life. The respect accorded very young children, not as future artists, but as human beings enjoying full potentiality in *all* areas of growth, is indicative of the kind of uniqueness needed in adult life for every human being, regardless of race, sex or belief, to make a worthwhile contribution.

Art *is* indeed for children. It is a very vital part of their preparation for responsible adulthood!

# Art Materials Guide

Young children should be provided with those basic art materials they can handle with safety and with full utilization of their creative powers. Chapter 3 discusses the use of art materials, both commercial products and those obtained at no cost. Chapter 4 explores the basic elements and principles of art while Chapter 5 combines both facets in developing meaningful art expression. The purpose of this section is to provide adults with concise information to enable them to purchase manufactured art supplies effectively and economically.

When considering the purchase of art materials for children, adults are urged to be fully aware of two major considerations. First, they should look for the CP seal of the Crayon, Water Color and Craft Institute denoting highest standards of quality and safety (see page 39). Second, they should recognize that top quality lines give greater economy and greater satisfaction in the long run. For example, the second quality or so-called "economy" lines of tempera paints have less brilliant hues, are less opaque, and cover less area. The same comparisons occur between top quality and cheaper varieties of other standard materials.

## *Papers*

In general, non-shiny surfaces are most effective for use with paints, chalks, oil crayons, wax crayons. Exceptions are noted for boxed watercolors which, because of their transparent nature, function more effectively on a *white* drawing paper which is not highly absorbent, and for finger paint which requires a special glossy surface. Papers packaged for school use are generally available in 50 sheet or 100 sheet packages or in a ream package (500 sheets). Of the standard 9″ x 12″, 12″ x 18″, and 18″ x 24″ sizes, the 12″ x 18″ size is recommended as the most versatile because it provides a suitable size for children's paintings and drawings and may be cut for other purposes. The following varieties are readily available:

> *Buff or Cream Manila.* Excellent choice for general use. Usually 50 lb. weight.

> *White Drawing.* Sulphite paper, 60 lb. weight, serves all media but is essential for watercolor for best results. More expensive but longer lasting.

> *Newsprint or Unprinted News.* Available in 100 sheet pads or by the ream. Especially suitable for experimental purposes. Is lightweight, less durable and yellows quickly. Sometimes ends of rolls are available from printing companies that print newspapers.

> *Construction.* Packaged in assorted hues or by single colors. Two qualities of construction paper are available so purpose should govern choice. The more expensive construction paper—100% Sulphite —possesses stronger, richer hues, does not fade as readily and will fold without cracking. The standard lines—Sulphite plus ground wood—serve many general needs where color brilliance and paper strength are less essential.

> *Poster.* Assorted color packages in lighter weight than construction paper.

*Art Tissue.* Sheet size 20″ x 30″. Available in single colors by the quire (24 sheets) or in assorted color packages of 20, 50, or 100 sheets. Paper quality and range of hues reflected in price variations.

*Finger Painting Paper.* Special glossy white paper, 16″ x 22″, available where finger paints are sold.

## Crayons — Wax

Top quality wax crayons offer more brilliant hues and greater ease of handling for young children than pressed crayons. They are available in large sticks (8 color) which are suitable for beginners. The more generally popular standard size crayons are available in 8, 16, 24 and 48 color boxes. The 16 color box is recommended as fully adequate for the needs of young children.

## Tempera Paints

Only top quality paints, liquid or powdered, are recommended as possessing greatest effectiveness and economy. Two forms are available:

*Liquid Tempera.* Sold in *sets* of six ¾ oz. jars, six 2 oz. jars, twelve ¾ oz. jars but not recommended for children as most practical.

Single colors are sold in 2 oz., 8 oz. (½ pint), 16 oz. (pint), 32 oz. (quart) sizes. Although ready mixed paint may appear more convenient, the problems of drying out cause waste and greatly lessen the over-all economy and efficiency in extended use.

*Powdered Tempera.* Sold in convenient one pound packages. Colors mix instantly so any quantity may be prepared as needed. Colors do not deteriorate in powder form and mixed paints keep without spoiling when covered. Recommended for greater long-term economy.

## Finger Paints

Although finger paints are available in powdered or liquid form, the liquid is far more satisfactory. The 8 oz. (½ pint) size is most practical. Children should use only *one* color until considerable experience is gained. Although nine colors are available, one seldom uses more than three or four at most.

## Watercolors

The transparent paints available in boxes are not recommended before age eight unless the child has had considerable experience with tempera paints. The use of watercolors should be a treat, not a source of frustration. If purchased, the box containing 8 half pans of color is recommended. The No. 7 brush packaged in most sets is too small for the most effective work. The addition of a No. 11 brush is strongly advised.

## Chalk

Soft, colored chalk offers variety for children. The word "pastel" is often used in the title to distinguish it from the harder blackboard chalk. Those chalks or pastels manufactured for children's use are less expensive than imported artists' pastels but serve children's needs fully. Available in 8, 12, or 24 sticks to a box. Paper with "tooth" or roughness is most suitable for use with chalk.

## Oil Crayons or Oil Pastels

These combine the soft, richness of chalk with the cleanliness of crayons. Boxes contain 12, 16 or 24 sticks per box.

## Markers

A special caution is necessary where markers are used. Avoid *permanent* type markers because of possible toxic fumes and difficulty in removing. *Water-soluble* markers, broad tip or fine tip of felt or nylon, are recommended for children.

## Brushes

Brushes used with tempera paints should be firmer than those supplied with watercolor boxes. Very suitable ones, labeled *Easel* brushes, are usually flat, wedge-shaped (rather than round and pointed) and are made of black bristles. Easel brushes generally have long handles. Practical choices are ½ inch or ¾ inch in width. Also available in round, pointed shape.

Brushes used with boxed watercolors are typically round and capable of forming a point when *wet*. The proper way to test the *point* of a brush is when it is wet, not dry. Small brushes do not foster the best painting. Typically they will be called "camel hair" or "squirrel hair" and the size 11 is particularly desirable. Larger size "wash" brushes (No. 14) are suitable also.

## Clay

The term "modeling" is usually applied to those clays designed for children. "Plastiline" and "Plasticine" generally denote those more costly varieties (generally imported) used by artists. Modeling clay can be used over and over. Self-hardening clays are not advised for young children.

## Miscellaneous

**Paste.** Children frequently need an adhesive for paper only. Small jars of white "school" paste or "library" paste serve such needs.

**White Glue.** Where greater strength is needed, white glue has become a staple in most households. Because standard white glue cannot be removed readily, it is recommended that the variety called *School Glue* be used with children. It launders out with soap and water yet bonds wood, paper, and cloth securely.

**Tape.** Kraft gummed brown paper tape offers a variety of uses besides package wrapping. Of the sizes available—1″, 1½″, 2″, 2½″, 3″—the 2″ width is most versatile. Such tape must be well moistened with a sponge, not licked, for greater effectiveness.

**Stapler.** A standard desk type stapler serves many uses and can be handled easily by children.

# Art Processes Guide

Throughout this book emphasis has been placed on providing experiences, materials, working space, stimulation and encouragement to enable children to develop their own creative capacities most fully. Often adults feel the need to visualize ideas and understand working processes before attempting to motivate and guide children. *The suggestions that follow are intended for adult guidance only. They should NOT be shown to children.*

## Designs That "Grow"

In Chapter 5 the concept of design was approached by an illustration of a "game" to stimulate children to utilize design as a means of *filling the entire space* of a given sheet of paper. The idea of growth can be applied effectively to diverse design problems, a few of which are illustrated here. Such experiences should follow extensive discovery of elements and principles of design as described in Chapter 4.

If we observe examples of lines across the page which children might produce with their eyes closed, we might see some of the following:

If we pursue the "game" idea, we need "rules" to follow. The first rule is to begin with the most prominent loop or part, or if more than one, to repeat the same design motif in each. The next rule is to let each additional line grow from a preceding line or part, never in isolation. The final rule is to extend the design until it runs off the paper. Children will develop their personal designs in unique ways but one line might develop as follows:

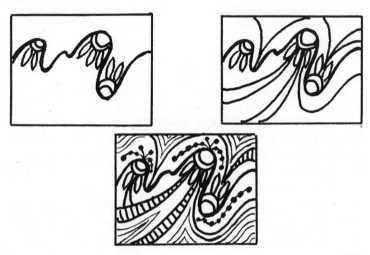

Such a design will be enhanced by *repetition* of shapes and colors within the design, by *variations* in texture, thickness and thinness of lines, and by *progression* from light to dark or alternation of light and dark hues.

Another approach to designs that "grow" might use flower and leaf forms. A few starting rules might easily set the process in motion with the final outcome dependent on the individuality of each child. One might begin by suggesting that the child draw with a light colored crayon three large circles on a sheet of paper making sure that they fill the space well but without any one being in the exact center of the page.

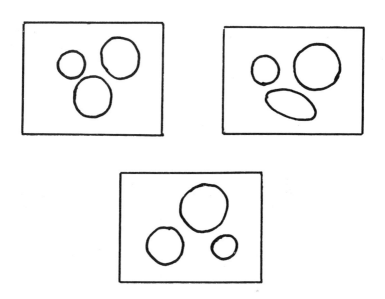

Next, encourage the child to develop each circle with many colors into an imaginary flower using various lines and textures. Complete the design by filling the entire page with leaves, vines, tendrils—all "growing" out from the flowers.

Likewise, a design could "grow" from the placement of a small circle for a head and a larger oval for a body into a fanciful bird, complete with elaborate tail, crest, feathers, and enhanced by a setting of imaginary flowers and foliage.

## Create a Positive-Negative Game Board

In Chapter 5, the principle of *positive-negative* is discussed briefly. Although many aspects of this pervading principle of design are too complex for young children to produce, children can learn considerably from playing with an easy-to-produce game board. Such experiences will also enhance children's understanding of the principle of *repetition* discussed in Chapter 4. The game experiences suggested here may pave the way for children to produce their own examples as their art expression matures.

### *Constructing a Game Board*

Materials needed are a piece of corrugated or heavy cardboard, 12 inches by 18 inches (precise measurements necessary), a piece of white or light, neutral colored felt or flannel, 16 inches by 22 inches, and masking tape at least one inch wide. Cover the cardboard with the fabric, lapping over the edges and taping securely on the reverse side. It is now ready for the following uses or others which may be developed subsequently:

## Expanding a Shape

Using a square or rectangle, cut shapes from the sides, flipping them over to create a positive-negative design. As additional pieces are cut *with no waste,* they reverse positions in more complex patterns.

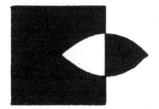 

For young children, adults may prepare a cut shape from heavy paper or felt to be played with on the game board until they are ready to explore their own original examples. Children may wish to paste their expanded forms on sheets of contrasting paper.

cut from felt or heavy paper for use on the game board

## Exploring Repeated Patterns

Adults need to prepare the set of "game pieces" which children will use in exploring pattern as follows:

> ● From a dark colored construction paper, make a set of 24 triangles by diagonally cutting 12 squares measuring 3 inches on each side. Precise measurements are necessary to fit the game board.

- From the *diagonal* edge of each triangle, cut out the *identical* shape retaining both the original triangle and the piece removed. These 24 triangles and 24 small cut outs are the playing pieces for several games.

- Use simple cut out shapes for introductory experiences, adding more complex ones as children gain experience and show interest in further development.

Preparing the game board for play involves an important first step. Always arrange the 24 triangles on the board in *regular grid* pattern to begin. The smaller shapes should not be used in the first games for they are apt to confuse the child. The single unit and first arrangement are as follows:

Each succeeding step involves flipping or shifting certain triangles in *regular sequence* to create diverse pattern grids. Many varieties are possible and, as a game, can provide children with enjoyment as they become conscious of design principles which operate universally.

*small unit added*

If children particularly enjoy the process, they can be helped to cut their own set of 24 triangles using identical design shapes. Adults can aid them by preparing the triangles from the squares making it easier for children to cut the design units. They may follow the play experience by pasting the completed design pattern most satisfying to them on a sheet of contrasting colored construction paper.

Another valuable experience for children following their experimentation is to search for examples of design grids used in various situations such as in wallpaper, flooring, gift wrapping and textiles. Although designs will take many other forms than triangular units, children can discover that the plan of organization is the same. Floral sprays, leaf designs, other units will be found to be repeated systematically.

## Folding and Cutting Processes

Many forms of art expression are accomplished more easily and effectively by direct cutting without previous drawing. Children should be encouraged to cut freely both when producing shapes singly or when developing forms from folded paper. If more than one or two folds are involved, paper should be very light weight. Scissors should be sharp enough to cut cleanly and of a size comfortable in the child's hand.

One of the most basic forms required is a *square*. Because young children do not know how to measure with a ruler, they need to learn how to obtain a square from any size rectangle. Grasping one of the lower corners of a rectangular sheet of paper, bring it diagonally across until the lower edge meets the opposite side evenly, fold from the corner across and cut away the excess strip.

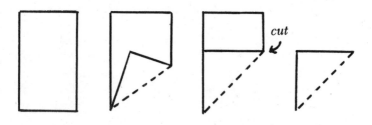

By folding the square thus obtained in various ways, one can cut varied designs readily. Children need to be reminded to remember where the folds are located, never cutting them away entirely.

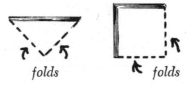

folds          folds

The snowflake discussed in Chapter 4 is somewhat more complicated to fold, but once children learn how to do it successfully, they will repeat the process endlessly. As in nature, so in cut paper—no two snowflakes are alike. Lightweight paper and sharp scissors are essential. Begin by making a square from a rectangle of any size as already diagramed. Fold again diagonally. Bring right folded edge one third of the way across to the left. Overlap left folded edge across to the right, adjusting in as even thirds as possible before creasing the folds. Turn over and cut across even with the visible straight edges of paper. Cut designs from each folded edge being careful not to cut entirely across. Open carefully to reveal a six-sided snowflake.

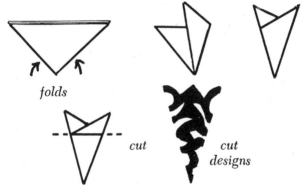

*folds*

*cut*   *cut designs*

## Construction Processes

Children frequently show great resourcefulness in constructing a large number of items to enhance their play. This same enthusiasm can be readily guided into artistic expression particularly if adults can help them develop more satisfactory processes toward achieving their ideas. The suggestions that follow are geared to simple, practical methods involving a minimum of expense. Adults are cautioned against purchasing costly hobby kits with fixed end-products which do not encourage children to develop their own ingenuity and self-reliance.

## Scoring and Folding

One of the most frustrating experiences occurs when children try to fold paper or cardboard that won't crease evenly. Paper has "grain" and often is observed to fold more readily in one direction than the other. Learning how to *score* paper or cardboard for accurate folding is a simple solution.

To score for folding, place a ruler or straight edge along the lines of the desired fold and draw a blade firmly but lightly along the line. Adults may use a *single* edged razor blade or razor type cutter but these are not recommended for children. A paring knife, pocket knife, or even a scissors blade will serve. The sharper the blade, the lighter the cut required to fold neatly without cutting too deeply. A little experimentation will help each individual accomplish satisfactory results.

## Cutting Cardboard

Because children's hands are not strong enough to cut cardboard with scissors or knife blade, they need other methods. In some cases, scoring cardboard as previously described on both sides, then bending back and forth will cause it to crack apart. Although the edge may not be as cleanly severed as a cut edge, it will often serve adequately. Another device children can use easily is a small *keyhole saw* which because of its narrow, open blade will operate readily on corrugated cartons and other cardboard.

## Attaching Techniques

Children are always happy when pounding nails with a hammer and will find this method satisfactory for some purposes. But not all surfaces can be nailed. Tape serves well in some situations but adults and children soon learn that they cannot cover transparent tapes with paint. Masking tape works better for some surfaces, but the most practical is brown paper (Kraft) gummed tape which must be well moistened with a sponge to adhere fully. White glue is a versatile adherent for many substances including wood.

Often children wish to adhere a form to a round tube-like structure. In this case, adults can be most helpful in showing children how to slit the edge about ½ to 1 inch apart, depending on the diameter of the tube, fold the slit portions inward or outward, scoring if necessary, and proceed to fasten to the additional form.

Creating a cone shape is simple once a child learns the method. Start with a circle, cut from one edge to the center (the radius of the circle), overlap the edges as far as necessary to achieve the desired conical form, and fasten securely. For a very pointed cone, one may need to cut out a wedge to lessen the overlap.

## Puppets

Various simple forms of puppets are discussed in Chapter 5 which could be exciting for children. In addition to simple stick puppets, there are countless ways to create hand puppets. The following suggestions are illustrative of methods that may be adapted and combined in various ways as children become involved. The most important guide must always be that children themselves are able to create their own puppets. If adults must do all of the work, the method is too difficult. A few hints and suggestions, plus occasional help on specific problems children face, must constitute the adults' role.

## *Puppet Heads*

The head is the most important element and may be made from many materials. Balls, rubber or Styrofoam, need a hole to fit over the child's finger for manipulation. A painted face, hair of yarn, rope, curled paper, a cap or hat, glasses or other accessories complete the puppet character's head. Another type may be made from a paper tube to fit over the finger covered with a simple cloth head. The cloth head is stuffed with soft material and shaped over the tube. A face is drawn in one corner of an 8 or 9 inch square of cloth, hair added plus other accessories prior to stuffing.

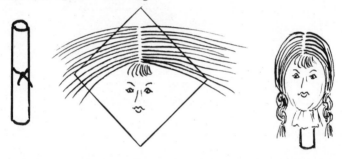

A very simple but effective puppet may be made from a paper sack. A painted face, some painted hair or curled paper hair can be quickly made. Curl paper by drawing it between your hand and the blade of a scissors.

### Puppet Bodies or Clothing

The very simplest consists of a piece of cloth placed over the child's hand before putting the puppet head over the finger. Later, as children become more experienced they can make simple garments of cloth to cover the hand.

In order to make trousers, a shorter top can be made and the trousers attached to the front of the blouse, thus dropping in front of the hand. Belts and aprons can be tied around the child's wrist after the puppet is put over the child's hand. The garments may be attached to the puppet head, if desired. Capes, scarves, and other items are easily added.

### Hands

It is often said that hands are important in creating certain characters. Both puppet heads and hands are generally exaggerated in order to more effectively denote the character. A mitten-like hand is easiest to make. More detailed hands, such as those with long, bony fingers can be created for a character such as a witch. Wire doubled and covered with adhesive tape for each finger, then wrapped together can create a very effective hand if needed.

## Papier Maché

One of the most versatile, yet inexpensive, mediums is papier mâché. The pulp form is not recommended for children generally, but the strip method has many possibilities. Essentially, one is dealing with a base structure coated with paper strips dipped in a paste solution. The easiest methods leave the base inside. More elaborate hollow forms, with base removed, are much too complicated for beginners.

The *base* or *core* may be created from paper sacks, boxes, cardboard tubes, rolled newspaper tubes, held together by string, brown paper (Kraft) tape, staples. Crumpled newspaper makes the lightest stuffing. Rolled newspaper makes durable legs but one must experiment to keep them as light as possible yet strong enough to stand. For example, an animal could be constructed of a large sack for body, a smaller sack for the head, and rolled newspaper for legs and tail. Use crushed, not folded, newspaper to stuff sacks. Tie legs in place with string using a figure 8. Use of a figure 8 form for tying holds securely without binding too tightly.

*Coating* is made of *torn* paper strips. Cut paper has a hard edge that will not blend when pasted. To tear newspaper easily, take a folded section of newspaper, place a yardstick or long ruler on top, grasp the *folded* edge and rip strips quickly. For most forms strips should be about one inch wide and 10 or 12 inches long. Tear narrower ones, about one-half inch wide, for smaller forms or details. For large surfaces, larger pieces of torn paper are often practical.

*Cover all working surfaces with newspapers.* Mix wallpaper paste or Metylan paste according to directions. Use a shallow bowl or basin for paste. Dip one strip at a time in the paste mixture, drawing it out between the fingers to remove excess paste, and begin coating the form. *Blend down edges carefully.* Tear and overlap pieces that project to avoid bulges or air pockets. Work in different directions to fit shape, overlapping strips. The first complete layer should be allowed to dry. If necessary, prop legs in jars, wad paper under projecting parts, or support in any way until the form is dry and rigid.

Once the first layer is dry, the process will become much easier. Bits of paper that did not dry properly may be torn, overlapped, moistened with more paste, before more layers are added. Usually 3 to 5 layers will be strong enough but one should judge the thickness according to the size of the object. If desired, the final layer may be made of *torn* paper toweling to give a more pleasant textural surface to paint. Even cloth can be added as a final layer. If a part is too flat, it needs more shaping after the first layer. This can be achieved by adding small wads of crumpled paper covered with more strips dipped in paste. Ears, tails, other details can be added in numerous ways and children will often be more ingenious than adults in fashioning such finishing touches. The object should be thoroughly air dryed before painting.

### Paper Bag Birds

Similar methods are used but a flat, envelope sack will work more easily for the base form. Starting with a flat sack that is 4 to 6 inches wide and about 7 to 9 inches long, stuff one corner to form the head. Use a small wad of newspaper to keep the head small enough. The corner becomes the bill. Fold in the excess parts of the sack after tying to form the neck. Stuff lightly to form the body, tie again and use the remainder of the sack to form the tail. Wings, legs, crest, and other details can be added as the paper coating is being applied. Prop as needed to keep shape and dry on waxed paper to avoid sticking.

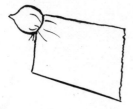